Field of Corns

D. D. Cross

This is a work of fiction. All the characters and events portrayed in this novel are either products of the author's imagination or are used fictitiously.

Field of Corns

Copyright © 2012 by D. D. Cross

ISBN-13: 978-1466400429
ISBN-10: 1466400420

I awoke this morning to the sound of cars clickety clacking along the steel drawbridge heading into the city. It was rush hour and the good people of the world pumped up on caffeine, mojo, despair, desolation, and desire, pursued what had once been an American dream. Good for them, I thought. I'd chosen to live under a bridge and drop out from all things the legit people considered wholesome, and live life on my own terms. They weren't particularly the terms an adult would advise their children to follow, but hey, they worked fine for me. Maybe I'd check my mail today it'd been a few weeks. Not that I was expecting anything, who knows? I could've won a free subscription to Modern Bum or Today's Scofflaw, a couple of magazines I'd submitted short stories to. Maybe I'd break into the world of literature and really make a name for myself. Yeah right, I'd have to quit my day job.

It was drizzling and a chill hung in the air. Judging by my shopping cart wedged between one of the girders and the concrete embankment, I saw that I was running low on Sterno. There was maybe half a bottle of wine left over from last night. I was still laying back staring at the underside of my sleeping bag taking in the rhythm of cars, soothing as it was, the sound of suckers heading toward a place I'd have been a spell back didn't quell life's hangover. I had to laugh inwardly though, these days, all that crap even the crummy headache didn't mean much to me.

I propped myself up on my elbows and looked up and down the street. In this part of town things, pretty much stood still after the highway shut down the exit ramp. The mom and pop stores were mostly boarded up. The gas station/convenience store remained open. It wasn't part of some large chain it was an independent shop that a third worlder ran. He sold goods for thrice the price to folks who lived from one handout to another. I wasn't cool with that, but that's the way the world works, right? I became friends of sorts with the boss. He had taken to American shoot-em-up-movies and after I supplied him with a cowboy hat and nicknamed him Buckaroo Bagwam, he and his bimmies treated me just fine. They always had some coffee, aspirin, and a newspaper, for me as long as I put on some good cheer, and looked after the joint when no one was at the counter, either taking a smoke, or in the crapper. No big deal.

Across the street was a mail order degree doctor's office. He was in jail, but the place was rented out to a crooked chiropractor, dope dealing dentist, and bent podiatrist, who rarely showed up. It was nestled between a massage parlor, shot and a beer bar, and some ancient jagoff triple X-rated bookstore. The porn shop mostly catered to the geriatric set who hadn't entered the digital age. Favoring grainy images of youthful models in pathetic poses for gramps to ogle. Billy Damiento the chiropractor, kept office hours every Monday, Wednesday, and Friday, from three to seven. And damn that place was always packed on those days. Of course the regulars in the hood peddled whatever they could. The dope dealers were drying up on account of the pill mills doling out drugs in semi-legit facilities all over suburbia. The hookers might just as well have worn neon logos, flashing open for business signs on account they hadn't seen much action since the highway barricades went up. Yeah, traffic flow to this side of town pretty much came to a halt...

Dostoevsky said that you can measure the degree of civilization in a society by entering its prisons. I think he had it all wrong. A visit to any part of a city whose lifeblood was human traffic and had its freeway exit sign removed from the main throroghfare was emblematic, and a far better metric of society. Every American city had sections of it like this one, and they were spreading fast. The American dream hadn't died, but it was on life support.

I stood up and stretched. One of the hookers, Nell, joined a pair of winos next to a flaming barrel for a few seconds, walked away and was standing on the sidewalk in the rain staring at me. Her makeup, like a faded watercolor, streaked down her cheeks. She wore a tight tube top that was soaked, nipples like agates and pair of dirty Lucite heels. She looked over at me and said: "Yo sleepy head, you got some juice?"

"Nell," I said. "It's too early for Sterno." She just shook her head.

I had just finished changing my clothes when the rain stopped. The sky began to clear and in the distance the sound of a badly tuned car puttered until it had come to a stop at the curb. I looked over and saw the rumbling rusting out nineteen fifty nine red Cadillac convertible, its top was down and a craggily faced man wearing a metal studded leather biker's jacket and a spread collar shirt was behind the wheel. The man driving had Elvis sideburns and a cigarette dangling from his lower lip. He was adjusting the rear view mirror while admiring and combing his thinning coiffure. He honked again and raised a container still in a brown paper bag, held it up in a toast of sorts and shouted out: "Hey what's up?"

He polished off his drink and tossed the empty on to the already littered street where it shattered silently. He grabbed a can of beer and went into bouncing back and forth to the music blaring from the car's speakers-Macho Man by the Village People. It was playing so loud the winos warming their hands covered their ears, and Nell the hooker shooed at the bloody red car with both arms. There were steer horns on the Cadillac's hood where an ornament ordinarily would have been, and after taking a long pull from the fresh container called out again:

"Hey, CP you wanna make some dough?" He wiped his mouth with the sleeve of his shiny black jacket. "C'mon, it's easy money." He had a merry grin, as if he'd just gotten away with something, which he probably did.

The man was Neal Grinder, M. D. a general practice physician who had his finger's crossed when he recited the Hippocratic Oath. Grinder is a doc who did the bare minimum to get licensed and never bothered with any area of specialization. He scoffed at board certification as a waste of time, and liked his freedom more than the responsibility that comes with keeping current in any particular specialty. He found himself unemployable in the twenty first century, and didn't care. Grinder never wanted to work for anyone but himself. He didn't want to open up his own shop, not because he couldn't, but because he didn't want the hassles that came with it. He'd say that he didn't want to be bothered with all the aggravation, administrative nonsense, headaches, paperwork, and competition, with the boarded crew, who DID obtain certification along with hospital privileges. Fuck `em, Grinder always liked to say. The chiropractors, physician assistants, nurse practitioners, or the lot who'd insisted and won by way of litigation, lobbying, politics, and flat out underpricing, came to rule the roost of general medicine anyway-why should he bother? There was no room for guys like Grinder, or in fact me either. I did spend a few years after medical school training in surgery and did well for a spell. After a few malpractice suits, actually more than a few, and a pair of divorces, I also said, fuck `em. As for Grinder, he dabbled in all sorts of things, many unrelated to that of a doctor.

I addled down the slope and put my hand on the passenger side of the car's ratty exterior. "Grinder turn that fucking music down!" I wasn't bullshitting. The street junkies, crackheads, and gang bangers, who'd been on the prowl throughout the night into the early morning were never too far away. At this time of day they'd be asleep, not particularly wanting to be disturbed.

"You're such a pussy Caddypod," Grinder said.

"What's the gig?" I asked, not really wanting to know.

"I got me some action at the nail garden and we can score a few bucks," he said. "Easy money. We just do a little routine care: a blood pressure check here, tweak a few diabetic meds, some incision and drainage action there, take over a few other cases, tend to some beds sores, some minor shit, and boom, we get well for a few hours work."

Grinder went back to bobbing his head to the music. "Easy, peasy, Japanesey CP."

A nail garden was a nursing home. A place where oldsters live out their final days. Some just lay about, drool, and mumble to themselves incoherrently. Most of the old folks were pretty much parked at these places while the families bickered about who'd be picking up the tab. The oldsters with unshaven faces on the men, grisly gams and hairy pits on the gals, all of them needing medical care beyond the scope of the nursing staff. Usually the facility would have a regular doc on the clock. Someone working for the individual home to come in and do the job, a pretty easy one at that. But sometimes a doc wouldn't be available. Their insurance would pay a decent wage for each gray haired head. Yep, in the teen years of the twenty first century the state would shell out enough money for a weeks worth of groceries to any kind of schmuck with a license to treat these fossilizing folks. All they had to do was make an entry into the chart. Easy coinage to do the grisly scut work, like cutting the oldsters toenails, or work through a dirty granny panty to look at an infected crotch. The places smelled of urine and decay and if you wonder what sorts would do this type of work, you'd be puzzled.

Often a kid fresh out of residency just starting out would be on the payroll, but they-the young docs-often had other plans, or an excuse not to do this shit. Most of time it was folks like us, independent contractors, guys like Grinder and I, we were those sorts of schmucks. Yeah, I recall thinking, that if time was money, the folks living in nursing homes were on their way to going emotionally bankrupt fast.

"How'd you come by this?" I narrowed my eyes and looked at the rascal. I had to be skeptical on account Grinder had his medical license suspended a few times in the past for various degrees of shenanigans. He once shared an office with a demented dermatologist diddling a disability claim. Grinder agreed to sign off on phantom procedures, and divide his cut with the soon to be indicted doc. For an array of reasons including but not limited to personality issues, an absence of clientele, and Grinder's tendency to inflate bills, the way a fisherman brags about the one that got away, that deal ended poorly. I just shook my head. and asked: "How're we going to get paid?"

Grinder leaned toward me and spoke in a hushed conspiratorial tone: "Zill's under investigation for fraud, and he's on the lay low, so he gave me a call and said I could use his office to do the billing. No big deal."

Zill Crapmonger was another general practice doc I was acquainted with. I was familiar with his personal and professional history which had a few gaps, a bunch of stains, and several stretches of unexplained holes. Rumor had it that Zill had spent some time in the joint for some offense or another related to a loose way with his prescription pad, and a lust for the ladies. Pretty gals were known to have left his medical office with a sense of being violated after a visit where he'd given them nitrous oxide gas for analgesia. Yeah, old Zill had an office downtown here, in this ramshackle part of the city that was largely abandoned. I didn't mention it earlier on account Zill only came by once or twice a month because he was being surveilled by John Q Law, and the gang bangers found him easy pickings for a few Percs, Vikes or T4s. Zill spent most of his workdays at one of the tit bars in the hood. He'd be sipping slow gins, and shoving dollar bills into garter belts while a recent residency grad worked his uptown office twenty miles, and a different world away. Yeah, you can take the street urchin off the street, but guys like Zill always found a way to zone in and cannibalize any crooked angle and cash in. Zill was ninety nine percent street, which didn't leave room for much else.

"Where is this nail garden?" I asked, mostly to confuse Grinder and get him to turn down the annoying music.

"You know I don't like to venture far from home."

"C'mon CP," Grinder said. "A change of scenery will do you good. This joint Zill turned me on to is out near Hoogerstown on the other side of farm country. It ain't too far."

"That's still a long drive from here," I said. I really wasn't into this gig. Any time you start putting bills into the system somebody somewhere is going to have you on the radar, and that's pretty much why I live under a bridge with no return address. The only things I own are in my shopping cart and I like it just swell that way. It keeps the ex-wives, bill collectors, and process servers, away.

"CP, don't sweat it. I'm driving, and I'm gonna do all the billing under my name and have the loot sent over to Zill's mail drop. You don't have to do jack shit but see a few patients, write a script or two, listen to some lungs, tend to some bed sores, and clip some nails. You scribble a few notes in the geezer's charts, badabing, that's it." He motioned for me to come along. "It's easy money, you still got you're narcotics ticket don't you?"

He was referring to my DEA, drug enforcement agency license, which I'd kept up.

"Yeah, I keep it in my wallet," I said, stepping away from the car. "But really I'd planned on heading over to the country club and doing a few loops later on today..." Catching a loop was caddy slang for carrying a bag. A double loop was when a caddy would carry two bags.

"Come on Caddypod the ground's still wet, and it will be all day. You know they've got plenty of carts and who wants to pay a caddy these days? Face it Caddypod, caddying is a dying profession." Grinder said.

"Hey Grinder so's general medicine," I said. "And it pays better." I knew that most people preferred a golf cart, but didn't really give a hoot. People who wanted a caddy carrying their bags wanted quality. They wanted expertise of the course, someone to rake the sand traps and shag stray golf balls. Someone they could bitch to about this and that, and then tip nicely to keep their mouth shut on account they'd be embarrassed for making damn fools of themselves for snapping an expensive golf club in half or tossing it the brush screaming for their own ineptitude.

"Get in. I got a sixer of brew from Buckaroo Bagwams, nice cowboy duds on the dude. I put it on your tab."

"You what?"

"I put it on your tab. Word on the street is that you're a real stand up guy for a bum."

"Hindu, Grinder, show a little respect for the folks who sell me beer and let me run up a tab. My tab." Sure enough there was a six pack on the tattered leather seat and I snapped one off, cracked open the flip top and said, "Eh, what the hell?"

"Eww, CP, you smell like a freakin' sewer, we gotta get you cleaned up. I know of a shower stall at a park along the way. There's some clean scrubs I helped myself to from the surgi-center in the trunk."

"You got it all covered don't you Grinder?"

"Hey, I'm your man on the street. I always stop by one of the surgi-centers to get coffee and a danish. I check out the surgeon's lounge, and see if there are any unlocked lockers for some uh, how you say...pocket change."

"Jeez Grinder you really are scum of the earth." I drank some beer and patted my jeans to make sure I had my wallet I always kept it with me. It had my driver's license, my medical license, and my good luck charm, an old Krugerrand. Don't ask me why I never broke down and sold it. Maybe I'm just superstitious, or it might come in handy some day if I got really desperate. I looked at Grinder with his Elvis sideburns and phony as a chiropractor's sales pitch grin, and said "really man, you're a real piece of work."

"And then some." Grinder shot a finger at me like he was pointing a pistol, cocked his thumb, and added: "Pow."

Grinder was the sort of guy whose body of work could be outlined in chalk. He had ghosts in his closet like most of us, but Grinder's ghosts, had nervous systems made out of the flashing neon lights that flicker in some of the planet's seediest shot and a beer bars.

"Hey Caddypod, we gotta get some blank forms, some dressings, scalpels, hemostats, and nail clippers. I friggin' forgot my shit." Grinder chugged the remains of his beer and tossed the empty can out the window.

"Why didn't you just get them from Zill's office in the first place?"

"Shit, I forgot Dammit." Grinder spit the words out "Dammit, dammit, dammit."

I knew that Grinder had other reasons to avoid going back to Zill's but wasn't about to mention it on account he'd just bullshit me. Maybe this little scheme wasn't sanctioned by the owners of the nail garden, maybe Grinder didn't get prior authorization. Maybe he was treading on someone else's turf? I didn't want any beef with The Organization.

It was too late to turn back. We were already outside of the city limits, and the skyline of Bigtown was a hazy shadow of tall buildings and bridges with some rolling hills in the background. It was a nice looking town from out here in the country, and I told Grinder as much. Grinder was fuming in that way semi-sober folks do when they don't get their way. "Cool it Grinder. I know an osteopath who works out this way. He'll loan us some gear for the garden, no sweat," I said, mostly to calm him down.

We were in the suburbs and the fringe of strip malls peppered with mom and pop stores, chiropractors, dentists, and legit doctors-all trying to scrape out a living sprang up less frequently the farther we traveled from the inner city. We passed a couple of hospitals and plenty of fast food joints. The more miles between Bigtown and its burbs the cleaner and more aesthetically pleasing they were. We went from gritty urban decay through lower, and struggling middle class communities along the way on our journey. Times were tough, but the real metric of this point in history could be told by the makes and models of cars, the people who drove them, and their various states of decomposition. I saw these things in the shopping centers, grocery store parking lots, and faces of the people on our way out toward Hoogerstown, a long ride deep into the heartland surrounded by farmland.

"Who's the D. O.?" Grinder asked. He had his head out the side letting the warming air blow through his mop of dirty brown hair. "Think he'll give me a few Vicodin?"

"Maybe," I said, shaking my head. As if Grinder wasn't already driving under the influence teetering on one license investigation or another. At least he had the sense to take the back streets and obey the traffic signals. Last thing he needed was a traffic stop. I looked around to see if there was any heat, nothing. I did notice a truck that seemed to have been showing up sort of regularly on our tail since we left the city and made note of it.

"Tommy Brassiter, he's got a family practice clinic out in the Boonies. You think you can pass a sobriety test?" I asked Grinder.

"Why? There ain't no cops. But shit yeah." Grinder looked puzzled and said: "Tommy's a D. O. now? Shit wasn't he a chiropractor or somethin' like that?"

"Yeah." I said. "Tommy wanted to write prescriptions and said fuck it. He upped and went to osteopathic school."

"How much did he have to pony up to get in?" Grinder asked.

"I heard forty K." I said and glanced in the side view mirror to see the truck that'd come in and out of sight along the way. "You think of any reason someone'd be looking for you Grinder?" I asked. Mentioning the truck that might have been following us.

"Nah." he said. "Ain't nobody followin' us. Tell me did he keep his back crackin' ticket?"

"I heard he let it lapse. But did you notice that truck behind us?"

"There ain't no truck and nobody's following us. Where'd you hear that, about Tommy?" Grinder looked in the rear view mirror then over at me and grabbed another beer. "So what's the deal with Tommy B, how'd you run into him?"

"A ways back at the Club. Tommy was on the links doin' eighteen and saw me there, and had me caddy for him and one of the other guys."

"No shit." Grinder sipped his beer.

"Yeah, there were three other Osteopaths, an ENT, an Orthopedic Surgeon, and another GP."

"Did Tommy give you any shit about you know...bein' a friggin' caddy?"

"Nah, he was pretty cool. He knew I'd dropped out of society and was doin' the lay low." I said, feeling around for my trusty can of Sterno. It was there. I always carry a can with me so that I can whip it out and act like I'm fucked up on the shit so nobody bothers me. It usually works.

"I gotta hand it to you Caddypod, you did manage to disappear-sort of fell off the grid. Who'd imagine a guy with your education be livin' under a bridge, hobnobbin' with hookers, and doin' whatever you damn well please. How much did you stiff your ex-wife for?"

"Hey Grinder, I haven't had enough booze in me to reveal all my secrets. At least not yet."

"I'd like to pick your mind about some of that shit. You know, CP, you don't show up on a whole lot of databases or anything, and if you do, it's all fugazi-shit. It's like you don't exist."

"No shit Grinder, it keeps the assholes and bill collectors away."

The flashing yellow light at the intersection of Interstate 895 and 341 must have been outside of Grinder's field of awareness. But there it was maybe ten feet in front of us pulsing yellow hard and it came upon us fast. There was no one on the country road and I didn't have a reason to suspect anything sinister'd be lurking, but just like a cold snap after a hard punch the big spooky truck was upon us and slammed into the Cadillac jolting us hard from behind.

"Go out and get his information before the cops show up Grinder. I think I got me a whiplash.

"The fuck Caddypod, we gotta split. I got some weed in the trunk."

"Let me handle this," I said. "You get rid of the empty beer cans and the shit in the trunk."

I approached the truck driver who was standing next to the cab shaking his head. He didn't look like an ordinary truck driver. Unless of course truck driver's were wearing disco era clothes with big gold chains and smoking Virginia Slims. He had a bad rug, and looked shaken up. His hands were on his hips and the smirk on his face made him look like he was sniffing dirty diapers.

"You look a little freaked out," I said reaching into my scrubs for the hip flask I'd carried in case of an emergency. This was an emergency. I opened it, and passed it over to the pansy driving the big old rig. He took it and drank.

"Ahh that was good," he wiped his lips with the back of his shirt sleeve just as the sound of sirens blurted in the distance. He handed the flask back to me and said: "Aren't you going to have some?"

"No," I said. "The cops are going to be here and I don't want to have booze on my breath."

"Well asshole, you and your buddy aren't going to be taking any business away from anyone today are you?"

"Who the fuck are you?" I said. I was a little freaked out.

I don't know what happened next, but my guess is the guy decked me.

I'm not sure how much time had passed until I came to, but woke up with an aching neck. I was laying on the side of the road and saw the Cadillac's crumpled trunk and exhaust coming out of the tailpipe. Grinder was staring down at me, shaking me, shouting: "Get up man, I don't know what you said to that guy but he jumped back into the truck after that left hook and looked pissed before he took off. Let's get out of here before John Q shows up."

"Grinder, that asshole works for <u>The Organization</u>. This was a set up."

"Get the fuck out of here Zill's no dummy." Grinder said. I knew it sounded too good to be true. Zill's <u>in</u> with <u>The</u> <u>Organization</u> and their crew. "He know's they don't like people messing with their turf, that's why he farmed this gig out to me." Grinder thumped his chest.

My vision was blurry but not too blurred as I climbed the ladder to awareness, looked down the country road and said: "If' you're sure this gig is cleared by way of Zill Crapmonger, let's just stop at Tommy's place and file an accident report."

"That's what I like about you Caddypod, you always know how to turn a buck. The trucker really did fuck up my car... By the way, how you feelin'?"

**ONE QUACK AND A SOCIETEL DROPOUT
GO TO AN OSTEOPATH TO GET TREATED
FOR WHIPLASH AFTER A BIG TRUCK
INTENTIONALLY RAMMED THEM TO
PREVENT THEM FROM FUNKINESS AT THE
NURSING HOME IN HOOGERSTOWN**

Tommy Brassiter D.O.'s office was a giant ranch home straddling three state lines. Instead of having a front lawn an asphalt paved lot lay in its place with more designated handicapped spaces than a Veterans Hospital. We pulled up toward the entrance looking for a space, it was packed. We drove past all the vehicles parked helter skelter. It looked like a used car lot for sick folks, and some bombed valet was on duty. The place was busy and there was no denying that old Tommy B had a booming operation.

"Jeez Caddypod," Grinder said. "Take a look at old TB's setup..." he was trying to find a parking space for the Cadillac and wasn't having much luck. We sat there with the engine idling for a few minutes watching the door for someone to leave when a pair of yokels came out. Two dudes with baseball caps on backwards, untucked T-shirts and jeans, dark shades, and brown bags, nodding at each other like they'd just scored. We followed them to their late model pickup truck. The punks stopped. One of them lowered his shades and stared at us like the wrecks we were, ready to be cannibalized. We might have been wrecks but weren't ready for the junkyard, not just yet. The yutz slid his shades back up his nose and clutched the bag close to his body. Maybe he had some drug samples that'd get them buzzed and figured us as a threat. Hell, I'd be suspicious of us, we did look like a pair of desperate men in a beat up rag top. The other guy touched Mr. Staredown, who shrugged, shook his head, and finally walked away. They got into the truck, high fived, cranked up the engine, revved it a few times and peeled rubber out of the lot. They opened up a parking space for us between a late model Lexus and a Jaguar Vanden Plas. Not too shabby. I was glad I didn't have to use Kung Fu, than again so were Kung and Fu whoever they were.

"Tommy's gonna really be surprised to see us, eh?" Grinder said getting out of the driver's side.

"Yeah, like a case of the clap on his honeymoon," I said.

"What's that supposed to mean CP?" Grinder said in a harsh, belligerent tone.

"It means that Thomas Brassiter was an osteopath with a legit office, real patients, and real responsibilities these days. And a pair of yahoos like you and me ain't got no business barging in on him before lunch without an appointment."

"Come on Caddypod, TB's a bro. He was a regular dude back when."

"Yeah, he may have been, but I got a hard time figuring out when back when was, but I do know this: people change. He did go to graduate school, got a doctorate in biochemistry and then went on to osteopathic school."

"Big friggin' deal. He had the scoots, paid off one of the wise guy osteopaths and got a seat at a D.O. school. The dude had an angle and played it. He might be an osteopath but he's still the same old crook he always was." Grinder said in that tone reserved for resentful twerps who wished they'd done something similar. As in taken a road toward legitimacy, but was too proud, and too ashamed to say so.

"You're just jealous Grinder. You could have done the same thing if you had the patience."

"Fuck you CP," Grinder said. "You just didn't want to pay alimony you cheap bastard, and you butchered enough patients didn't you?"

I locked eyes with Grinder and held his gaze in a way reserved for someone about to be rained on hard. I must have stared with such intensity that after a few beats he held up his hands palms open and said: "Okay, okay I get it, we all make our choices. You made yours, I made mine. Let's just skip it. We cool?"

I relaxed a bit, took a deep breath and let it out. "Yeah, we're cool."

The facility had pride of purpose at the intersection of two roads in the middle of farm country. The single story behemoth looked like a hospital, military installation, and low rent motel, rolled into one osteopathic medical center that catered to one and all. The double door entry had the name "Dr. Thomas Brassiter" bigger than life plastered on it in orange dayglo letters. You'd have to be blind, stupid, or remarkably stoned, to not get it, sort of like the pair of twerps who'd given up the parking space. It was a doctor's office. The waiting room was shoulder to shoulder packed, standing room only. Every Tom, Dick, and Mary, from podunk who the hell knew where, waiting to see the great Tommy Brassballs. Osteopath to the hicks, junkies and well insured. Yeah, Tommy was a smart kid back in college, but knew greener pastures's lay ahead with the right tools. As in getting a Ph. D., and then a D. O. degree instead of settling for a chiropractic diploma and limiting himself to being an O doctor. As an osteopath he could do everything as far as doctoring went and wouldn't be breaking the law by prescribing this or that, and examining a nice pair of tits as well. You might want to know what an O doctor is. That's when someone introduces themselves as Dr. so and so. Psychologists, chiropractors, dentists, and podiatrists, they're O doctors. If they aren't doctors of medicine or osteopathy people have a general tendency to say "Oh."

I went up to the pebble glass window and slid it open to say hi to the receptionist. She was a bespeckled fiftyish woman sporting a flaming red beehive hairdo, and more chinchy jewelry than a thrift store yenta. Her name tag read Trixie, and she pushed her glasses up her nose and looked at us the way a store detective looks at would-be shoplifters.

"Hello," I said, mustering up my best fake smile. "We went to school with Tommy...tell him Caddypod and Grinder are here."

"Do you have an appointment?" She said flatly.

'Not really. But he'll see us," I said.

"What is this about?"She asked.

"We're a couple of old buddies and were in the neighborhood-I'm sure he'll find the time, Trixie. We're MDs how about a little courtesy?"

She sneered, shook her head and stared at us before saying: "You two are physicians?" In that snotty trenchant tone often used by check-in clerks at high end hotels, or car salespeople at dealerships who're really saying that you don't look like you could afford the price. I've heard it enough times to recognize the sort of creep who sizes you up, pigeon holes you, sets the spirit, usually not a good one, that characterizes the way you'll be treated. I also learned to say-fuck `em all.

Grinder a man never known for keeping his mouth shut said "Lady, we went to school with Tommy and we're old pals! Jeez, I'm an emm dee, so bug the hell off."

She had a puzzled look on her face like she'd just discovered that the toilet paper she'd just taken a swipe with was really emery cloth-extra coarse. Her mouth was shut and she drew her thin lips into her face before she spoke. When the words came out they sounded the way people do when they're choking. "Do you have an appointment Mr. Emm Dee?"

I jumped in quick. "Trixie, I told you, we're old friends, we went to school with Tommy," figuring this snarky bitch would lighten up. She looked over at a computer screen and held up a pudgy finger.

"Let me check the schedule," her voice had a grating unpleasant tone as if she was too busy for us.

Well fuck you too, lady. Her face was awash from something. Maybe more than the glow of the machine, it looked a bit too flush-maybe she'd been surfing the web-checking out some internet porn. It wasn't a pretty sight.

We stood there watching as if her Ben Wa balls had rubbed her wrong. She saw us stare, blushed, and went to the desk top to rifle through some papers. Real busy huh? I thought to myself. Busy like a bee. Fucking asshole.

"Okay, let's have another look," she said wiping the spittle off her chin from spitting out her last sentence and went into shuffling papers. She still had that pretentious dilettante thing going on, and played it up swell. Why rock the boat, I thought as I just grinned and waited for instructions. After a minute she stopped, sighed, and told us what to do next.

"Take a seat, I'll tell the Doctor you're here, Mr..."

"That's <u>Doctor</u> lady," Grinder said sharply. "<u>Doctor</u> Neal Grinder and <u>Doctor</u> Cad E Pod. Get it?"

She shook her head, "Excuse me <u>Doctors</u>. Take a seat." She stared hard at the two of us, like she was an antibiotic and Grinder and I bacteria. Don't worry sweetheart we won't scuzz up the joint. I thought, but; didn't want to cause a stir. That was Grinder's job.

Something told me it'd be a long wait. I picked up an ancient National Geographic and walked over to the aquarium to stare at the Angel Fish. Grinder sat down on the floor in front of the big screen TV switched the channels to some cartoon show and cranked up the volume. It was just loud enough to get a nasty look from the broad behind the window who slid it shut with an audible thump. There were a few hems and haws about his obnonymity from the patients in the waiting room but Grinder ignored them. I tried to distance myself from him and just wondered what Tommy Brassiter's monthly overhead was. The aquarium took up the better half of one of the walls of the waiting room and the fish in there looked like they came from all parts of the world. Thinking back, so did the patients. They were an odd mix of folks. Many of them genuinely ill farm folks, but most of the population seemed to match the fancy cars in the parking lot, all bejeweled and well dressed. A higher class of dopers, like those two truck drivin' punks with the brown bag and baseball caps. Oh yeah, they had on more gold chains than a pimp in the heart of Bigtown.

Tom Brassiter let us see a few patients at his office. After all, I was licensed in one of the three states his ranch style office complex straddled. I could see a few of them in one, and Grinder, shit, he had licenses in all three. I got to wondering how Grinder managed to keep active licensure in all three states. I knew the states he was licensed in had three separate practice acts with three regulatory boards to lose, misplace, or reshuffle complaints, or court orders which I knew Grinder had plenty of. If enforced, that meant that as a far as Grinder's issues went in one state he could work on a person while supervised, another unsupervised, in the third who knew? It was confusing but Grinder always could bullshit his way around things.

Tommy B was board certified. It was a different sort of Board Certification on account the word Osteopathic was mandated by its respective boards. Tommy didn't give a shit.

He knew that the Board Certifications of Osteopaths wasn't like the Board Certification of Medical Doctors. Osteopaths were generally under the umbrage of the American Council of Graduate Medical Specialties, or the ABMS, the American Board of Medical Specialties. Add in the word "Osteopathic" to those and you've got mainstream medicine. Lots of people say that guys like Grinder aren't real doctors, and some take that real personal. They said the same thing about osteopaths a few years back, but that somehow changed. Maybe it was the shortage of doctors in the US, or the fact that the state of California let osteopaths trade in their D.O. degrees for M.D. degrees. It really didn't matter if you were an M.D. or D.O., the mainstream clubs would let you in. Chiropractors were verboten.

Shoot, Grinder liked to say that osteopaths didn't have the grades, or MCAT (medical college admission test) scores precluding them from getting into an American medical school. Touchy stuff for the osteopaths who insist that they love their nuanced folksy ways, and that writing D.O. after your name added a certain quality to the practice of medicine. Every time I hear that I gotta laugh. The osteopaths- end up spending more time explaining what those letters mean. D.O. sure they'd be every bit as legit and working the same as any M.D. and making the same dough. D.O.'s had their own clubs, and just as there were M.D. specialists there were the same D.O. specialists. Only they had to write D.O., I always thought it sounded dumb and looked shitty on a letter head D.O., do or do not. Eh, that was just me. I was an M.D., Orthopedic Surgeon, and D.O.'s no matter what they did or how they did it do were just stuck in some semantic abyss. But ask a board certified dues paying member of the national or state association about these things and they'll throw a hissy fit. Shh...you didn't hear it from me, but they say osteopaths aren't R. D.'s (real doctors). They are.

How do I know this? Well, when I went to medical school and got my M.D. degree I spent a few years as a medical and surgical intern and resident. I learned the difference between D.O.'s and M.D.'s was to some, like that of being a professional athlete. There were the pro wrestlers in the WWF, the

D.O.s, and then the real pros, the NFL-M.D.s. Osteopaths are good posers, but there was a time when they were like chiropractors. Chiropractors really don't know what they don't know. That's OK with me, nobody really gives a crap unless someone gets hurt. But that's a whole different story. Hell, some chiropractors have gotten jobs in Orthopedic surgery groups, not just fetching coffee, but actually doing adjustments or manipulations. Things that the Orthos didn't have the time to bother with. For the most part chiropractors set up their own practice's and slog about building it up. After few years of groveling some do OK. Some do very OK. I had a chiropractor working in my old clinic who made a ton of loot. I didn't let a lot of other docs know that I hired chiropractors on account this would cut down on my referrals and increase hassles. Lots of M.D.s are like bitchy little girls, and run to the state board to file complaints over the size of a Yellow Page ad if they think you're making more money than them.

That being said, me and Grinder were considering seeing a few of Tommy's patients on account he was as busy as he was. I said what the hell and went on to see a few folks with bum knees, twisted fingers, torn rotator cuffs, and some sprained ankles, till about noon. Grinder was nancing about from one treatment room in one state to another treatment room in another. He couldn't practice in 3 of the 9 exam rooms. I could only work in one of the three rooms in the state I had my license in. The office had that sense that if the music "Flight of the Bumblebees" were piped in, it'd be just right.

Finally, when Trixie told us it was lunchtime we heaved a collective heavy sigh. Old Tommy B had us sitting around the giant consultation room table that sat smack dab in the trisection of three states. Shoot, Tommy's desk was half in one state, half in another, and me and Grinder sitting across from him were in another state altogether. Fortunately the one Grinder chose was the seat in the state with the highest threshold for blood alcohol level for being drunk or impaired. Oh yeah, I didn't mention that we were supposed to be drinking non alcohol beer, right? I lied.

"What are you mulanjan's up to?" Tommy asked, putting up his clog laden feet sans socks and torching up a Winston. His office was as state-of-the art as it gets. Every gizmo medically imaginable was there. And they served pretty much as cash registers as they did diagnostic devices. Yeah, Tommy was raking it in. Maybe the canary yellow Aston Martin

Vantage with the vanity plates reading O$teoDOC said something about the pudgy D.O.

Thomas Brassiter was really Thomas Brassiterio, and despite the fact that he was a doctor of osteopathy he still had that chiropractic edge. The defensive, territorial edge that made sure the handful of patients seen between Grinder and myself were listed, the procedures performed spelled out, so he could collect full fee. He made us wear white coats with no names on them so the patients couldn't recall who treated them for what, and the prescriptions for heavy meds were delivered lickety split. TB knew how to build a practice and giving everyone some narcotics worked well. He was the regular tri-state go to guy for a quick fix. Of course Grinder hit him up for a box of Vicodin samples-Me? I'm a Sterno man. Never touched the stuff, but today, eh, I popped a Vicodin.

Tommy Brassiter dressed in a way unlike most men who reflected a certain level of achievement, status, or what Tommy would describe as class. It amplified his personality and for some would have shone a light on him as stylish or at least trendy. But Tommy? He was probably the only doc in the country who wore a leather biker jacket, an expensive one, to see patients, and his hair slicked up like Elvis. He was a real contender for worst dressed man in America. He made a point of holding up his right hand and extending his pinky finger equipped with a semi precious stone of sorts to punctuate most of what he said. Yes, Tommy like Grinder, was a trip, along the lines of one might find at a run down amusement park. A rickety roller coaster came to mind as we told Tommy about our mission to the nail garden and being rammed by a truck. He'd already speed dialed a personal injury lawyer and had us fill out a few forms so that when they found the truck who hit us, there'd be a case for us to cash in on. One of the states the office straddled had generous personal injury laws, and getting whiplashed was like winning the lottery. It also justified TB treating Grinder with drugs and some hokey manipulative therapy that took a whopping thirty seconds. Tommy was a crook, but we were colleagues of sorts. He'd gone to college with us, was a frat brother and the esprit de corps was there, but something was off. I couldn't put my finger on it nor did I waste much time considering his un-Tommyness on account he'd grown up and had a legit career and patients to deal with. He bid us good wishes on the way out. He also warned us about messing with the terrain of <u>The</u> <u>Organization</u>.

<u>The</u> <u>Organization</u> made it's name as a powerful, not to be messed with entity. A lot like some sort of Mafia. There were rumors and tales that spread the way spook stories do around campfires uttered in doctor's lounges, and privately among docs who've had a brush with the law, or an issue with the DEA. But they didn't have a Yellow Page listing and couldn't be Googled. They were not a real tangible company, just something that was there usually when you didn't really need someone or something poking into your business. They were a shadowy oufit that encompassed organized medicine in many of the states. A group who were tied to everything from outpatient surgical centers, hospitals, and nearly all the nursing homes, with underbid contracts, and managed care plans to work for below market prices. <u>The</u> <u>Organization</u> took young docs fresh out of school, and residency, and put them to work. Promising to cover their overhead and repay student loans and raked in scads of money. Money the youngens would only see a small fraction of.

Tommy reminded us that we'd have to come back once a week for the next month. He grinned and winked. "That's right, you will be in here three times a week for therapy. "He said it as if it were a dirty little lie that we agreed to, and shared a certain commonality in our hatred of "The Man" vis-a-vis the insurance industry. The lie that it was just a scam to keep our personal injury case going, but we all knew we wouldn't, and were sure he would just bill the car insurance company anyway.

So we left and bid farewell to our old schoolmate Tommy Brassballs ostepeopathic Elvis impersonator, and proud owner of one fine motor vehicle we'd admired on our way out of the lot. It was just past noon and the sun had cut through whatever crumminess the day started out with. Grinder had tossed back a pair of Vikes and I was a little concerned about his driving, but not too concerned that I'd offered to take the wheel.

"Hey Caddypod, why the fuck'd you drop out in the first place? Huh? You were makin' some good scratch and had it goin' on...was it the old lady? You know the alimony and shit?"

"Something like none of your freakin' business douchebag," I said gruffly. Maybe I envied

Tom Brassiter's set up, knowing I could've been running a gig like that myself. But after a few minutes of watching the rows of corn fields, the sun on my face, the fresh country air, I was actually grateful that all that stress of running a practice sucked. Maybe seeing a cool car still turned me on and I wanted it on some level, but I just didn't want to pay the price. I settled back in the cushy leather seat and looked over at Grinder. He was a regular dude, just wanted to make a buck, get laid and have a good time. He also dug seeing patients and doing doctoring. He'd been married before, twice. Both of them shrews who'd taken him for every cent he'd had. But he managed. After all like me, he liked girls. Actually a certain kind of girls...sluts. And both of us had been busted for cheating on our spouses in one way or another. We had to pony up some loot and lose contact with our kids and all the crap that came with modern divorce and scorned women. Grinder just paid and paid, while me? I cheaped out and took the assholes route and dropped out of society. There were just too many complexities that frankly, I didn't want to deal with. Call me what you want, but I did what I needed to keep my sanity. What I did, was go back to a trade I picked up in high school that paid well enough to get by and still be able to chill. That was caddying.

The thing about being a Caddy is that it teaches you humility. You deal with a lot of uber wealthy folks who throw tantrums, golf clubs, and abuse the crap out of you, and you pretty much don't have any recourse but to say: Yes sir, no sir. Try the two iron, tend the pin and rake the traps. There wasn't much need for caddies in the teen years of the twenty first century, but; the super exclusive country clubs had a certain clientele who insisted on 'em. To some, having a caddy was sort of like a personal slave. And with the increasing self-conscious craze to be in shape, golfers took to walking and talking with each other rather than zooming about in electric carts. I was lucky in that the country club I caddied at all those years ago had a caddymaster who recalled the good old days of golfing. When I filled out my ap he saw that I was a doctor and it piqued his interest. I explained that I was going through a divorce, fed up with practice, and I was going to lose whatever I had in the bank. I could handle a double loop-no sweat (double loop means two golf bags at a time). So the caddymaster hired me and I took my place in the little cubby a few steps below ground level beneath a canvas awning on one of the wooden benches with the other caddies waiting for their turn to go out for a round of golf. Usually eighteen holes required a bit of energy. I guess that's why the caddy shed, not to be confused with the movie with Bill Murray, was part of the country club. In fact it was beneath the sumptuous dining room and was really the backroom of the elaborate golf shop that had the expensive clubs, clothes, and accoutrements, for the modern golfer. There was a door leading out to where the caddies hung out. One of those two part doors that opened at the top and bottom, painted white over knotty pine, like something from another, simpler time. It had a bottom door and a sort of bar or ledge where the caddies could step up with the players cards to be reviewed by the caddymaster, and the caddies could sign off on the scores. The ledge also served as a place where the caddies could get energizing snacks and beverages. There was no liquor allowed and the caddies could yack, yammer, and bitch to the caddymaster, AKA the crumb boss. Especially about the tips they either did or did not get, and for how much or how little those tips were. As far as the other caddies, they came from all walks of life. There were street bums and winos who were just hanging out to make a buck or so, they didn't get too many loops. Nobody wanted a smelly no-nothing caddy who couldn't tend a pin. We'd often indulge in card games and the lower echelons of caddydom, the aforementioned bummery and boozehouds played fast and dirty. Nobody liked card cheats and the old adage, never trust a drunk even though they apologize again and again. The junkies were worse-they'd apologize while picking your pockets. But they were a minority. There were the lifers, guys who'd been caddying for decades and could tell the slope of a fairway, the condition of the grass and knew more about the course than the architect who designed it. These guys did not participate in games of chance, idle chatter, small talk, or sporting games other than golf, and often could be seen staring off into space contemplating who knows what. I could only guess it was the nuances of the weather, the wind, the clouds, and the miraculous pristine beauty of nature itself. Some of these lifers were like monks of a sort with a kind of wisdom that transcended the ages. To the rest of the world they-the lifers-were just caddies, but for those of us on the inside, they were gurus with the sort of inner peace and awareness that could perfectly sense the universe. Who knows maybe they could move mountains with their minds. And then there was everyone in between from high schoolers, college students, and a female, from time to time would show up. But for the most part the caddies were males. Most of the golfers were high powered folks. Attorneys, lobbyists, politicians, some physicians, and plenty of businessmen, who could afford the stiff dues. They used the Club as a place to make deals, discuss strategies, and enjoy nature in a casual environment, where sometimes someone's guard might be let down and things ordinarily unspoken came out. There were a few women golfers in those positions, but the old notion that big business was an Old Boys Club pretty much remained what it had been. The ladies, golfing in foursomes often opted to use the carts and their motivations were more along the lines of passing the time and enjoying an afternoon or morning with their friends. And there I was, Caddypod.

"Hey Grinder," I said, "sorry I snapped at you," I said as we drove down that open road toward Hoogerstown on our way to the nail garden.

"Fuggedaboutit," he said. The Vicodin must've kicked in. "You didn't want to deal with the bullshit man. I can dig that, CP." Grinder hiked his right hand off the steering wheel and pointed a thumb toward his chest. "Man, can I dig it, and today, we score at the nailgarden!" He put his hand back on the wheel honked the horn and shouted, "Yee haa!"

I grinned and nodded. When he chilled a bit and got back into the lull of driving and the buzz of the dope, I figured I could get a word in, and said: "Yeah, Grinder, I can dig it too."

We were driving for nearly a half hour and the farmland seemed to go on forever. The two lane highway looked like something out of an old movie with the immense cornfields on either side. There were few if any cars on the road and the occasional slow moving farm vehicle would come upon us only to be passed until Grinder sort of functioned on automatic with respect to using his turn signals and such that I started to doze. My head ached after this morning's run in with the semi, and the drugs from TBs office would have been wearing off if they did anything in the first place. The pills from Tommy's must have been expired or something on account they didn't alter my sensorium at all. Nope not one bit. I was just tired and at that point I didn't want any drugs or booze or anything. Not from TB, or Grinder, or anyone. Like I said, I'm a Sterno man myself. I was thinking about the celebration we'd be having after a clipathon at the nail garden and the good green dinero we'd score after all the corns, calluses, and nails, had been shalooped when I fell into a deep sleep. I dreamed, and they were vivid violent dreams about The Organization and its mythical monstrous machinations which engulfed medical practice from the heart of Big Town. Were they gangsters? Yeah you could say they were. These people were capable of almost anything and they'd stop at nothing to maintain their turf. The fact that notions of The Organization had come up earlier that day bothered me somehow especially in my dream. I imagined that whoever was behind the wheel of the big rig that rammed us-could in someway really be tied into The Organization.

I don't know exactly how long I'd slept but had awoken to the sound of Elvis Presley singing Viva Las Vegas and with my aching head it wasn't satisfactioning me. I reached for the knob on the radio to turn it down.

"Hey what're you doin', man? That's the King!" Grinder stopped drive boogying and looked over at me with an arched eyebrow. "What's up Caddypod, have a good nap? Shit, you slept for nearly a half-hour..."

At that Grinder yanked the wheel. A truck had pulled up alongside us and went into some serious horn honking. At sixty miles an hour on a deserted highway trucks coming out of nowhere have a way of giving you a serious spooking.

"The fuck!" Grinder said yanking the wheel hard to the right sending us off the road onto the swail toward the cornfield. We could see the back end of the truck, a dark eighteen wheeler. Its break lights were on as it slowed down and we could see the mudflaps with pictures on them. Grinder planted his foot down hard on the accelerator throwing a plume of dust and grit from the birm we'd driven up on. "Motherfucker's run me off the road, I'm gonna kick that son of a bitch's ass!"

"Grinder," I said clutching the dashboard. "We don't know who's driving that truck, and by the looks of things it looks pretty much like the bastard that rammed us this morning. Just get the fucking plate number and we'll put it in the accident report. Shit I'd rather have a few easy bucks than get in a beef with some Litvak truck driver."

"How the fuck you know he's a fucking Lithuanian?" Grinder said, still fiercely accelerating the Cadillac.

"It's just an expression, dude, we don't need this shit we've got to get to the garden."

Grinder eased off the gas and the Cadillac-fell back to a more non-hostile position behind the truck, which was beginning to make a turn.

"The fuck's that trucker doing?" Grinder said, slowing the Caddy down.

"It looks like it's turning around," I said.

"Shit, Caddypod. It is."

We watched as the tractor trailer backed up, jack knifing its cab so it could align itself on the highway. Finally it just sat there beyond the mirage spots on the road. They looked like puddles of oil or water and we could see its headlights glare and hear the mammoth engine roar like some angry jungle beast ready to surge toward us. Black clouds of exhaust fumes rose from the shiny metal stacks on either side of the cab whose windshield's mirrored tint job reflected the mid-day sun like the sunglasses of some vicious mechanized State Trooper telling us we were both: "In a heap a trouble."

"Shit Caddypod!" Grinder said.

We proceeded in the direction we were headed hoping, I guess, to have just passed the now oncoming truck as if nothing had happened. But somehow we both knew that wasn't going to be the case.

The truck had gotten into our lane and was barreling toward us, flashing it's lights, tooting its horn. Shit! We were on our way to a head on collision.

At the moment of our inevitability Grinder cranked a hard right and the truck hit the tail end of the red Cadillac sending us spinning into the field of corn.

I don't know how much time had passed but the sun was still near its zenith. It was warm and I felt something on my face thicker than sweat, and wiped off the moisture, shit, it was blood. I was on my back, maybe ten feet or so from the Cadillac. A real wreck, pale smoke was rising from the hood area and the door facing me was scratched along it's side and the front end crumpled. Grinder...where the fuck was he? I gathered myself slowly making sure everything was working, toes, fingers, arms, legs, my vision was ok, nothing felt broken and I started to stand...dizzy, achy, but overall I'd survived. I was all right, but for what I'd later discover to be a laceration just above my hairline. Grinder was slumped behind the wheel. I approached carefully, there were gas fumes and I didn't know if the vehicle might blow up. I shook him gently and eased him away from the steering column. His neck wasn't broken. If it was, I guess I may have just left him for dead. So much for my moral compass. But that was then. He moaned inaudibly, cursing something or other as I dragged him out of the wreck, laid him down in the cornfield far enough away from the Cadillac, that if it blew, we'd be safe. I sat there with him taking cover among the stalks, not knowing if the truck was going to come back and take another pass at us. I watched the stream of smoke from the car climb into a cornflower blue sky and disperse in the afternoon's thermals which kicked up to a one and a half on the Beaufort Wind Scale.

What the hell was that all about? Twice in one day...nah it couldn't be a coincidence. The moments passed slowly and there was no sign of the truck returning. After a while the rustle of a slight breeze whipped through the rows of corn like the sound of small children whispering along with the chirps of birds and other ambient noises of nature, was all we could hear. There was no wheeze from the wounded wreck, no explosion, it had simply plotzed. It lay there like some relic of the past, a beaten down soldier at the end of a long campaign settling back for a smoke. But the white plumes had turned dark and finally stopped just as Grinder began groaning: "Hey, where are we?" His voice sounded like he was speaking from the bottom of an oil drum. His eyelids twitched for a spell, finally opened, and shut, and ultimately opened again. It took some effort but when he could form a sentence, it was: "I need pain pills, lots of `em, and a drink, a double."

Three warm beers and a pair of Vicodin later, Grinder became a bit animated. Maybe it was the tincture of time more than the pills and booze. I say that because looking back, the beer was pretty low octane and the Vicodin seemed anemic, rather odd in its effects. It didn't give me a high or a buzz, just an unsettled feeling which I rode out and went with, and the sensation either wore off or got drowned out by the potency of liquor or the stupid snort of Sterno. I never really drank the shit-damn that could kill you—but once you whipped it out, whoever had some good stuff would offer you some of theirs. As for Grinder, drugs and booze, no matter how strong, hit his empty guts and got splurged on up through his greasy liver and on up on past his blood brain barrier.

That'd knock an ordinary person out cold or stop a charging bull, but that wasn't the case for Grinder, he was hard core and layed there qvetching about one thing or another, sipping beer and popping pills till we were well into mid-afternoon. I sat there staring at the sky, the occasional vapor trails of jetliners and the tranquil sounds of the field. When Grinder finally decided to get up off his ass he went into yammering, and started ruminating about how grand a set-up Tommy had and that he could've done just as well. Yeah, Grinder was fine. He was sounding like his old asshole self. We decided to forge onward. To where? We decided that the truck that was on our asses. would probably still be out there...somewhere on the highway-maybe waiting for us-and agreed that whoever it was, didn't want to buy us a round of drinks, or join our fan club. We figured it best to venture on through the cornfield, find a farmhouse, or the next thoroughfare, and make our way back to Tom Brassiter's osteopathic clinic. After all we did have a license tag number.

We had been trudging through the stalks of corn for over an hour, swatting aside the long stems like we were in some bad jungle movie of the last century only we didn't have any machetes.

"Dammit Caddypod, I'm friggin' tired of this shit. How far is the next road?"

"Nice to hear you're still bitching, Grinder. How the fuck am I supposed to know? You could've died back there in that wreck, you know that!" I was a bit aggravated, sweaty and painfully sober.

"You could have at least snagged the meds and the rest of the beer from my car."

"Fuck you, Grinder." He stopped swatting corn stalks, stood erect and planted his fists on his hips. "I'm sick of this shit." He had both faux Gucci loafers firmly planted in the soil far enough apart to indicate that he was itching for a fight.

"Asshole," I said, mimicking his posture and pointing a finger at him. "You're the motherfucker who got me into this. I could've gone over to the club and caddied if I needed the money. I hate fussing with diabetic medications and clipping toenails at the damned stupid nail garden."

"Well fuck you! I did YOU a favor, this was supposed to be easy money-asshole!" Grinder just stood there. "I ought to kick your ass Caddypod."

"Kick my ass? You probably scammed Zill Crapmonger into letting you do this gig at the nail garden and dragged me along so you could pin the blame on me. If, and it sure does look like a very real if, The Organization didn't green light Zill to farm this work out in the first place, asshole."

At that, Grinder lowered his clenched fists and his facial musculature slackened. He averted his stare upwards and to the right, then to the left before saying: "I didn't really have Zill's actual blessing. He owed me some money and I told him that I'd just go and make the monthly rounds at the nursing home and keep the proceeds. Maybe he wasn't exactly happy about it..."

"You double crossed Zill Crapmonger? You KNOW he's part of, The Organization. Do you really think ANY schmuck can just go and drum up a gig at a nursing home or out-patient clinic. Steal someone else's patients, inject some joints, drain an infected boil or bed sore, or clip ten nails and get away with it? Shit, Grinder, that was one fucking asshole maneuver if I've ever heard one. And you dragged ME along with you?"

"I'm sorry Caddypod, really. I didn't know they'd try and stop us."

"Yeah, what do you call that duo of dubious freaking accidents in one day, dickwad?" I jabbed my finger into his chest. "Those were deiliberate man." I'd lost my temper and was ready to deck the motherfucker, when...

Grinder's head notched upward with a jolt and he hollered: "Caddypod, what's that fucking sound?"

I heard a buzzing that grew louder with each beat of my amped up heart and looked up. There were some high-flying jetliners and maybe something else. I squinted skyward but didn't see anything right then, but could hear the steady drone of a gasoline engine. "I don't know, some sort of low flying plane?" I said.

We were both looking toward the sky and saw a biplane whoosh over our heads. It came in so low I could see the pilot's face, and it's wake made the tops of the stalks quiver, making them sound like an angry surf. It seemed to stall, and then we heard a loud hiss and we hit the dirt hard as the biplane let out a thick cloud of orange gas.

"Shit, it's a fucking crop duster!" I said, wondering what toxins were in the colorful curtain that draped us.

"How come we're in the only part of the field getting dusted?" Grinder shouted over the plane's roar as it left its load and we watched it gain altitude.

"I don't know, but I don't want to be here when, or if it comes back." I was on my feet, watching the plane as it banked hard to the right and straightened out. It WAS coming back toward us.

"Shit, we gotta move Caddypod!" Grinder was coughing.

I had my shirt hiked up over my face so I'd have some sort of filter. The air was like breathing mayonnaise. I called out through the haze, "Grinder what kind of a mess did you get us into? If we get outta here alive I'm gonna kick your sorry ass until you can't think anymore."

We had broken into a sprint through the thick corn rows, trampling the plants not thinking that the plane's pilot could see the trampled plants from above. He knew exactly where we were. We'd maybe run twenty yards when the sound of the biplane was roaring toward us like a locomotive. We surged forward when the rapid rat-tat-tat of machine gun fire sliced through what was already a deafening sound. "Shit!" I yelled out. They're firing on us..."

The ground in front of me got splattered by hot lead that sizzled, and phfft phftt phfftt'd before emitting debris and smoke. I dove into a thicket of weeds among the corn stalks, grabbed my knees up to my chest and watched the biplane throttle up and climb. The fact that we'd gotten strafed by a crop duster didn't sink in until I heard the moans of Neal Grinder.

He was a few yards a way and I could see from where I was balled up that he'd been hit. I watched the plane bank, heading toward us again for another run. I crawled toward my comrade in arms as the biplane made its approach.

"Grinder," I called out. "They're coming back. We gotta move!" I said.

I'd just gotten to Grinder, watching as the plane made its descent. He'd taken a bullet from the last run and his left leg was bleeding. I tore off his belt, made a tourniquet and tied it around the flesh beneath his knee. "I'm glad you know your shit Caddypod, I just wish you had some narcotics."

"Shut the fuck up, Grinder, these fuckers are on their way for another shot at us."

I looped his arm over my shoulder and held him up by his waist. I'd figure we make a run for it just as the plane dove, and a hail of gunfire splattered the earth again. This time way off target and the plane-let loose another plume of thick orange, maybe toxic gas.

"We gotta move, Grinder, we gotta keep movin' or the fumes might kill us." I said lugging him through the thick stalks.

"Or they come back and get lucky with another volley from their fucking machine gun..."

"Look," I said, watching the plane climb. We had both stared at the yellow biplane gain altitude and begin its turn. I heard the engine cough, then sputter. "Hey, Grinder, did you hear that?"

"Hear what?"

"The plane misfired, it's either low on fuel or they've got some engine trouble."

We watched its wings wobble from side to side, jinking I think they call it. It seemed unsteady in the air and there was dark smoke coming from the tail area.

"Shit, Caddypod, what do you think it is?"

"I think we're not as fucked as we thought we were."

The plane seemed to stand still for a moment, and then, something odd happened. The atmosphere seemed to have taken on some sort of charge. There was a strange electrical scent and my arms, legs, and eyelids, felt heavy, heavier than ever. It felt as if gravity had vectored in and tripled its strength, not just here among the stalks of corn, but in the air space above this field of corns. We watched the crop duster fall to the earth, maybe a mile or maybe less away. Seconds later there was an explosion and a thick stream of smoke rose from the earth. I felt my knees give out and fell as everything faded to black. The last thing I remembered was the smell of manure, fertilizer, or some other fecund stench.

The stars shone brightly amidst a field of wispy clouds, and the three quarter moon illuminated the cornfield in which Grinder and I had lost consciousness. We'd been rear-ended by a gypsy eighteen wheeler, run off the road by a semi, and strafed by a crop duster, on what started out as an ordinary day of schniding about. Who knows how long I'd been out, maybe Grinder had a better notion as to how much time had passed. By what I'd seen, the world had changed. "Grinder," I called out. "Where the hell are you?"

"Caddypod! I'm over here. Taking a pee in the cornstalks. Can you believe how clear the air is?"

I hadn't gathered my thoughts to have taken in the unusually clear air quality, but it did seem different in some way. At that time I couldn't discern why or how, but there was a certain quality to the atmosphere that had changed. On what would be a usual evening in the springtime the sight of airplanes, jets, criss crossing the sky were absent.The airport was not far from the highway between the city and Hoogerstown and I recall the sight of scurrying jets as they seemed to have blended in with the stars. Tonight I studied the sky. No planes, not a one.

"Hey Grinder, did you notice anything different in the sky?"

"I just got up and I'm friggin' hungry. You think I'm gonna look at the sky?"

"Forget it Grinder. What time is it."

I watched Grinder approach beneath the moonlit sky. His silhouette looked ghostlike as he approached tapping his wristwatch. "Damn knockoff Rolex, friggin' stopped working at two o'clock, and the date thing is stuck between days."

"Nothing like a fake watch," I said. "Better to have a real watch that works than a fake watch that doesn't work you moron. Let's just forge on and find some grub" I said.

"We can eat corn," Grinder mumbled, grabbing an ear off the stalk and peeling it.

"Schmuck," I said. "Remember that shit the crop duster dropped? I ain't eatin' that-No way," and began a trek toward civilization.

THE OTHER SIDE OF THE EDGE

I don't recall how far we travelled but judging by my aching feet and Grinder's incessant whining as the booze and pills left his system it must have been a few miles. We'd finally reached the edge of the cornfield and from that place I peered out onto a highway devoid of street lamps or the usual network of telephone wires. A simple two lane highway across which were a few telephone poles with one line running parallel to the road, and what appeared to be a small town. This was NOT Hoogerstown. This was a town that somehow looked artificial in the way a movie set looks, slapped together to fit some particular time or place. Maybe I thought, it was just me and our strange day, but pointed it out to Grinder.

"Eh, Caddypod, it's just a little old town in the middle of nowhere. Maybe it's an Amish town or something like that."

We were walking toward the dimly lit array of buildings that seemed even more old-fashioned the closer we got.

"Maybe," I said hesitating.

When we finally got to the town, things were indeed odd. There were only a few cars on the road and all of them were ancient. We're talking late fifties, something like that. There were no large chain stores and the sidewalks were deserted. There was a movie theatre, the old fashioned kind, all glitzy with flashing lights surrounding a white background with big red letters. On the marquee was the name of the premier feature film: "Cat on a Hot Tin Roof".

The ticket booth was abandoned and there were some film posters in the alcove leading into the theatre.

Bridge on the River Kwai, Peyton Place and South Pacific...damn, where the hell were we?

It wasn't more than a few minutes before a lone policeman walking what I suspected was his beat, came into sight. He might have kept walking but saw the two of us, dressed in filthy scrubs, flashy jewelry, jogging shoes...I looked at my reflection in one of the display boxes that housed upcoming movies. I saw my face next to the words Ben Hur coming soon and shook my head. Where the fuck were we I asked myself just as the patrolman approached us. He wore a khaki outfit, dressed like an old time paramilitary rent-a-cop, with his Sam Brown patent leather belt and shoulder strap. He could have been out of central casting as an aging

Barney Fife with a neatly trimmed white mustache and matching hair poking out from beneath his cap. He began tapping his nightstick on the palm of his hand.

"And what are you two young fellas up to this evening?" He asked in an accusing, yet friendly tone, as if we were troublemakers of sorts. He looked us over taking in our attire, posture, overall presentation, and finally staring hard into both of our eyes in the flickering neon light. Maybe it was the filthy scrubs we were wearing and Grinder's fake watch, gold chains and horse shoe pinky ring that made him arch an eyebrow.

"Is that blood on your trousers there, son?" He pointed his stick toward Grinder's leg.

"He hurt himself out in the cornfield," I said.

"You two don't look like you're from around these parts. The matinee's been over for hours. Maybe you can tell me what you're up to?" He used that interrogatory tone applied primarily by law enforcement types, high school assistant principals and others who wield power. He scratched the side of his head and said: "Those are some pretty funny looking outfits you have on. Dirty too. You with the carnival?"

"We got lost in the cornfield and an airplane shot at us and then dropped a cloud of dust on us and ..." Grinder stepped toward him spewing out the words so fast spittle sprayed the patrolman.

"Take it easy fella," the cop stood his ground. His face tightend up like he had a stomach ache. He wrung his hands in that way people who get spit on do, pursed his lips, narrowed his eyes, and began to slowly shake his head from side to side.

"Cool it, Grinder," I put my hand on my friend's chest to quell his panicky rant. Jeez did he have a big mouth. When he finally shut up I said to the policeman: "We're just lost officer, my friend's injured, and we haven't eaten all day. Maybe you can help us out?" I mustered my most humble, lost, and needy, voice.

The patrolman in khaki took a step back and put his hands on his hips. "Yep, you fellas do look a bit pent up and run down. The diner's closed."

We were clearly strangers, probably criminals, but trespassers nonetheless. And Grinder's baffling tone made the policeman edgy. He looked like he was thinking but couldn't figure us out. Two men in their late thirties give or take a decade, both in reasonably good shape, possibly athletic types, roustabouts or troublemakers. I could see why he might have some concerns as to the what or why we were where we were at.

"Maybe we ought take a walk on over to the station and sort out where you fellas oughta be," he said in a manner sounding more like an order than a suggestion. "We don't get many stragglers 'round here. Maybe the Sheriff can figure things out for ya'all in the morning. We got a nice empty cell on up the way."

"Are you arresting us?" Grinder struck a defiant pose and questioned.

"Arresting you? Nah, I reckon you boys are just lost, and old Nel's is booked because of the Pie contest."

"Old Nel's?" I said.

"She owns the town's Inn."

"My friend here could probably benefit from an ED visit or a doc. Maybe you can point the way?" I said. "Isn't there a hospital in Hoogerstown?"

"Hoogerstown? Ain't no such place. There's Hooger Lake, but that ain't gonna be there long becasuse of the dam they're fixin' to build."

"So there's no hospitals or ED's anywhere near?" I asked, figuring we could grab some food and a change of clothes. Fresh scrubs would do, as well as a cot to crash out on.

"ED? What the hell is that?" The lawman looked puzzled.

"Emergency department. You know the emergency room at a hospital?" I said.

"You boys sure ain't from 'round these parts. Nothin's open this time of night. Ole Doc Beaufort's probably half in the bag and what the hell is an ED? I think you boys best come with me. We got some fixin's down at the station," he said. "Maybe we can muster up a change of clothes for you too, after you clean up."

We both shrugged and let the officer direct us toward his headquarters. It was hard to believe this cop would take a pair of strangers and help them out. I guess that's where the old Protect and Serve expression came from.

"Hey Caddypod," Grinder whispered. "You notice that cop didn't have a walkie talkie or any electronic gizmos?"

"Yeah," I said. "He also was packing an old police special instead of a Glock. The guy was right out of a 1950s movie. I glanced back at him, wondering if I should ask him what year it was but thought better not and decided to just follow instructions. After all this could be just a dream.

I awoke in a jail cell not particularly clear about what happened the day before. My head ached a bit and my neck was stiff. I was wearing a flannel shirt and a pair of jeans that were baggy, very baggy. I heard the cackle of a radio and the sound of a song about <u>Volare</u> and sat up. The friendly policeman from the night before was seated behind a desk and I could smell the coffee. Grinder was in the cot next to mine and was still asleep.

"Good morning officer," I said as I stood up and walked over to the cell 's metal door that swung outward. To my surprise it wasn't locked.

"Hey young fella good mornin' to you." He was cheerful and one of my jogging shoes was on his desk. "I ain't never seen nothin' like these before."

He said, holding up one of my Nike's. "Go on and help yourself to a coffee and have a seat young fella. By the way, I'm deputy Barns. Jerry Barns."

"I was wondering what happened to my shoes." I said.

"You can call me CP."

"That must be short for something," he said, but I could tell he was mesmerized by the jogging shoe.

"They's really somethin'. I wouldn't mind takin' a stroll in `em. You get them over in Big Town?"

"Something like that." I said taking him up on the offer for coffee."

"Tweren't more than ten minutes went by after you boys shoveled down the left over Rice-a-Roni, cleaned up and pretty much fell asleep. Must've been a heck of a day, huh?" He put down the shoe.

"Rice-a-Roni, the San Francisco treat," I said under my breath.

"Yep." He said, grinning, just as the radio blurted out the first few notes of a Hard Headed Woman by Elvis Presley. "They just put that out, Rice a Roni. Good stuff. Lots better than that Elvis the pelvis." He hitched a thumb toward the radio, an RCA plastic job with a long antenna.

"The King," I murmured offhandedly, sipping my coffee.

"King of what? I don't know what the kids see in that fella. He ain't gonna go noplace with all that ruckus. And now they all got that Cha Cha dance. Kids." He shrugged.

We sat silently for a few moments as the song ended and the first few bars of Tequila came on. The deputy shook his head and turned the dials of the radio trying to find a station. After a few twists of the dial and the hiss and blurts of different stations the news came on and he leaned toward the radio. "Shhh, listen to that..." he was intensely listening to the broadcaster. A newsman describing how the first nuclear submarine, the Nautilus had just crossed the North Pole underwater. "Can you imagine that?" he said. "Ike's gonna pin a medal on those fellas. Can you imagine what the Ruskies are up to?"

"My, what an age we live in," I said.

"You got it CP, they already put a satellite up in space and they even got that Assa set up to keep the score even with the damn commies."

"NASA, deputy Barns. The National Aeronautics and Space Administration," I said.

"Yeah. That's it. Hey I called Ole Doc Beaufort for your buddy over there. I saw that leg of his when he got out of that monkey suit from the carnival and put the duds on. Looked like he got clipped by somethin' out there."

"I think he hurt his leg loading a truck or something." I thought it best to let him continue to believe we were with the carnival. "We were just working part-time for the carnies," I said.

He narrowed his eyes, leaned forward and put both hands on the desk, palms down. Shit. He probably thought we were communist spies or some other miscreants. Maybe there was NO carnival and he knew it. We very well could be fucked. Maybe he called the Feds, seeing the space age shoes...maybe he read the word Nike and thought we were...

"OK I fed you guys, got you some fresh duds now you gotta come clean with me. The sheriff's gonna be here soon, so's Ole Doc Beaufort. You gotta fess up now and tell me the truth..."

"Tell you what?" I hoped he didn't notice my face turn an ash white.

"How come nobody manages to get a coin to stay in them platters at the coin toss?"

At that moment Grinder joined us and said: "Cause we spray oil on the bottom of the pans."

"Hoo wee. You guys are sneaky. That's how you do it," he slapped his thighs with both palms.

I breathed a sigh of relief and was just about to greet Grinder when there were three firm knocks on the door. A man carrying a medical bag walked in. He said: "Good mornin' Deputy," his voice carried with a certain resonance reserved for holy men or people in positions of power.

"Hey Doc Beaufort, these are the fellas I told you about." The Deputy stood up and held up his cup. "Care for some coffee?"

Doc Beaufort waved a hand in that cursory manner suggesting that he didn't want any coffee. He set his bag down on the desk, planted his hands on his hips, and looked us over. He seemed to have a presence of sorts as if he owned the room he was in, probably any room. Sort of like a movie star or professional athlete, but no, there was something about him that commanded respect. Even Grinder, who didn't show respect for anyone dropped his merry grin for a moment as the man named Doc inspected us. It seemed as if he was looking right through us and the same time sizing us up. Evaluating our place on this earth and calculating what was to be done.

After what seemed like an eternity he said: "Well well well, we've got us a wounded leg and some fellas who look like they're a long way from home."

I looked over at Grinder and and motioned my head slightly so's to indicate for him to keep his mouth shut. Maybe the Doc saw me make the zip `em up sign with my hand across my lips, maybe not.

"They're carnies Doc. I told ya on the phone they were lost in the cornfield, this one's got the bum leg," He pointed at Grinder. "And this fella, he got these here fancy shoes, you gotta check `em out," Deputy Barns said.

"Carnies, huh?" The Doc pursed his lips and nodded slowly. "I think these boys ought to come on over to the office and get a check up."

"You're good, doc," the deputy said. "They ain't under arrest or nothin' and hey, you're the Doc you know best."

"These boys will be fine. Milly will fix them up a good breakfast and I'll give the Sheriff a holler when I got something to holler about."

We walked out into a beautiful spring morning and I swear the air had never been more clear and fresh since my earliest recollections of these things. I glanced back at the police station. The big wooden double doors, the adjoining buildings, and mom and pop shops, everything looked like it was out of some Norman Rockwell rendering of reality. I had to bite my cheek to check if I was dreaming. Doc Beaufort tapped his walking stick on the perfect sidewalk and led the way, taking in the marvels of this quaint town. The trees so neatly manicured, the automobiles shiny, and I gotta say this, it was like a scene out of the movie Field of Dreams and we'd been transported through time. But this wasn't a movie...we HAD been transported through time and something somehow told me that Doc Beaufort was in some way part of it.

Doc Beaufort's office was on the second floor of a row of shops in a freestanding building that took up an entire block. You could see from the sidewalk that there were offices up there on account of the painted windows with the names General Practitioner, Chiropodist, Dentist, and Osteopath. There was a plain wood framed glass door between the hardware store and a ladies dress shop. Each side of the door opened to a small lobby with an elevator that had an out of service sign and a staircase leading up to the professional offices.

Doc Beaufort held the door open for us and said: "Go on boys second door on your right, up top the stairs."

His waiting room was what some folks would call quaint but it looked like a comfortable den at a rustic bed and breakfast. The waiting room chairs, maybe five or six as well as a sofa were comfortable looking and there was a wooden table with a glass top with current copies of Look, National Geographic and Life Magazines. There were fresh flowers next to the receptionists window and an attractive woman with a peaked white nurses cap. She smiled at us as we moved toward the entry to the exam rooms and the inner sanctum of Doc Beaufort.

"Hello Beauf," the pretty lady said, and turned to us. "Hello gentlemen, welcome to our office. Can I get ya'all some fresh coffee or tea?"

"These boys need some nourishment Milly. Maybe you can fix up some eggs and toast," he said kindly. "If you aren't too busy that is."

"No problem, Beauf."

When she stood up Grinder nudged me and his merry grin was back as he ogled her remarkable figure. White stockings on a pair of long thin legs leading up to her perfectly starched uniform up to the red cross pin on her top.

"Cool it Grinder," I whispered. "Didn't you see the third finger on her left hand and the way she addressed the Doc? That's probably his wife."

Doc Beaufort led us into his private consultation room. It looked like what a private consultation room of a country doctor one would imagine would look like. Dark wood panelled walls with diplomas covering almost every square foot. A wall of books, and an x-ray view box displaying someone's hand on the side of his huge mahogany desk. It was strewn with papers, journals and a banker's lamp. There were all sorts of gadgets, some of which I hadn't a clue as to what they were. The obligatory stethoscope, otoscope, and opthalmoscope, were there but there were a few devices I'd never seen... very odd looking things at that particular time in history. Doc Beaufort motioned for us to make ourselves comfortable in either of the lush wing client/patient chairs in front of his desk. Behind us were even more books and a leather sofa. The place smelled like a medical office compared to the cloyingly sweet smell of the dentists office across the hall or the foot powdery smell of the chiropodists office next door.

Doc Beaufort sat down in his oversize leather chair with a whoosh and leaned back and stared at us. After a few beats he leaned forward and grinned. He had both elbows on the desk, his fingers forming a cage beneath his chin. He checked over to our left to make sure the door was shut and said: "Well, well, well, I know that you boys have come from another time. I saw you staring at the gravitometic evolunator on my desk. So you've probably gathered that I'm not exactly from around these parts either. Now just what you plan on doing here concerns me. So let's chat..." He leaned back, giving us the stage.

"What the hell is a gravitometric evolunator?" I asked, leaning forward. Grinder was to my left in the seat close to the door to Doc Beafort's inner sanctum.

"Yeah what is that mumbo jumbo? And who the hell are you?" Grinder asked sharply and went back to fiddling with his pinky ring.

"Well, well, well, boys. I am just what I look like I am. I'm an old time country doctor."

"Yeah, right," I said. "From what time and what country?" I thought I had the wily old coot nailed and then it occurred to me that he really wasn't wily and I couldn't discern his age.

"You are pretty sharp CP. That is what they call you CP, isn't it?"

"Yeah, his name's Caddypod, but if you're into the whole brevity thing, CP works. Tell him Caddypod..."

"Shut up, Grinder," I said.

Doc Beaufort picked up the device-the gravitometric evolunator-and said: "This here tells me when there's a shift in gravitational fields and one of the space-time portals out there in the cornfield opens up. You probably don't know about the portals, but after the cell phone wars of the 2020s they started popping up all over the place. Some folks'd just jump in and they'd go floating away into one dimension or another and that wasn't too good at all. No siree. Then one day some very smart person had the idea to put trackers on time jumpers so they could find out where they were going."

"Why?" I asked. I didn't know if the guy was bullshitting or not, but we were in 1958 and he sure as hell wasn't from around here.

"Well you see CP, things were so rotten after the wars that people didn't have much to do by way of makin' a living, goin' outdoors or doing pretty much anything. They would just jump time to get a new life started, and would land wherever they ended up. For a while that worked fine, but there were some paradoxes. In some cases not all, like you used to see in the movies people can not CHANGE history. They can travel back in time but if they try to change what has happened they're somehow frozen.

It's a strange thing, like if you were to go back and try and shoot Hitler. For some unknown reason, despite all those fine and fancy physics principles your fingers would lock up or something like that. Seems like there is some immutable law of the universe that you can not change what was. People got sick or died in awkward places, that sort of altered the course of human events. Anyway back to those trackers. They started tagging people so that at the moment of their death, they'd get drawn back to their own time. Some smart fellas came up with that notion and it made sure that the future stayed the same. By then many of the portals were identified to specific times and places. Say you were in China and wanted to come to this place here...well you could just jump into a portal and voila here you are." He made a sweeping gesture. "But you boys don't have trackers. You're here by accident."

"So what's with the cornfield?"

"Well the gravitational field and such of this latitude and longitude makes that cornfield a place filled with portals, hundreds of them. Heck, you fellas could have been back in ancient Rome or fighting lions in a coliseum with those get ups you had on. But that cornfield with all those portals is governed by some pretty strict rules of nature and one of them is, that when one of the portals opens this here gravitometric evolunator goes haywire and tells me that there's a shift of sorts and somebody's popped on through a portal. My job here, is to scoop them up and get them acclimated, and to make sure they've got trackers."

"Whoa, whoa, whoa, Doc Beaufort, does that mean we can't go back to 2012?"

He had a puzzled look on his face, held up the device and said: "Why in the world would you want to?"

"Maybe we dug it back then," Grinder was standing up, clearly agitated.

"Now, now sonny, sit down and listen up. You CAN go back or you can go to just about any place in history. But there are rules. You can't just pop into one time or another without a reservation. You can not just show up at some time and place without the proper preparations or you can end up putting history in the crapper. That's why Time Vacations and Time Share -Time Travel' is big business. In fact if you visit a time and place and want to resettle, that's an option too."

"Resettle?" I asked. Beaufort arched an eyebrow, leaned forward and spoke in a hushed tone.

"Lot's of folks in the future are not particularly happy with the way things turned out and simply move. It isn't cheap. But it's more fun than a trip to an amusement park or a condo at some resort."

"So we just find a portal, jump through it and we're in another time and place, huh?" Grinder said.

"It is not that simple boys." Doc Beaufort said. "The super duper computations need to be made as well as the genetic modifications and of course the residue issues have to be addressed."

"Residue issues?" I said.

"When you fellows went through that portal in 2012 you left a layer of sloughed off cellular material in the cornfield. Sort of like a snake shedding its skin only a teeny weenie layer." Beaufort held his hand out and made a pinching sign with his fingers.

"Why cornfields?" I asked.

"The corn slough mixes with the tissues you've shed and nixes any genetic material behind so there's no trace of a time traveler's DNA left anywhere they've been. Cornfields make for optimal neutralizer zones."

"So we's just gotta go over to the cornfield and feel around and we can go where we gotta go. That's cool."

"Grinder, I don't think it's that simple."

"No, CP. Not that simple at all. Before a portal opens there has to be a series of events like the tumblers in a lock so to speak to open up the door through time and space. The precise calculations are done by the computers and then you need to wait for the sequencing. OK, and then before the opening occurs a specific audio frequency has to go a humming and then the portal opens and you are good to go. But you have to have the right tones, the right keys if you will, to ride the harmonics of history."

"Harmonics of history?" I must have had a weary look on my face.

"Either we're dreamin' this shit or it sounds like we hit some cosmic cornfield jam session and did a mambo to get here. I wanna go back." Grinder held a knuckle up to his mouth, bit down on it and looked over at me.

"Shut up Grinder," I said, knowing he wouldn't.

"You two being here could very well be a freak occurrence. You see, there was a set of audiodynamic confluences that stuck the chord sending you to this zone. Heck, if you would have trampled through that field another few notes in a different key you could've ended up in dinosaur times..."

"Notes?" Grinder barked out. "I didn't hear no music. There weren't no angels playin' harps. A freakin' crop duster was flyin' low, shootin' at us, lettin' out poison gas. Shit, I got shot. I can still hear the sound of the plane and the gunfire and the engine dronin'."

"Well, well, well, it sounds like there was some confluence of tone and you boys may have been triangulated to be here now, or it was pure dumb luck." Beaufort rubbed his chin. "There is something very unsettling about this."

"Shit, talk about unsettling, look at Grinder's leg. He got shot for Christsakes!" I said.

"Oh, I wouldn't worry about an injury that happened in the future."

"My motherfucking leg, it..." Grinder looked at where he'd been shot then glanced over at me.

Doc Baufort said: "Grinder raise up that pant leg and take a look at that wound." He held his hands up palms facing outward. "I'm going to tell you boys a story."

"I hope it's a short one. I don't want to come down with some good old infection, Doc." Grinder said.

"The particular sounds you heard caused a resonance of the valence electrons and subatomic particles in such a manner to open the particular portal you passed though, delivering you here. As far as that leg, go on, take a look."

Grinder and I stared at his leg. It was healed, as if nothing had occurred. "How the...?"

"Simple boys, out there in the waiting room you passed through a scanner I had installed to reverse tissue damage. It's the medicine of the 2070s some fellow invented a tissue rejuvenator and wound reversal beam. Sort of turned back the hands of time. Heh heh heh."

"Say what?" Grinder said.

"In the future Grinder," he said, smirking and bobbing his head like one of those bobble headed figurines and said through a deep rolling chuckle: "In the future fellas, there are no doctors. Only nanotechnicians to set up and maintain the rejuvinators. People stop aging and there isn't much disease at all. Then again the cell phone wars triggered a whole new era of innovations what with the outbreak of brain tumors. I think it was a Dr. Thaddeus Bung who came up with the first angio-neoplastonal nanometerics. He'd come up with a microscopic, and I mean we're talking Angstroms here, devices that would just seek out, destroy and repair any misguided cells waxing toward the old cancer. Sort of made a lot of folks infertile. Then a few fellows took it, nano-technology that is, a bit further. Even won themselves a Nobel prize, the Zeeneyman brothers, yep. They went and reversed the aging process by tampering with cyclic nucleotides on the subatomic level and going so far as to...wait, let's see what you boys know about the DNA ladder?"

"We get graded on this?"

"If you'd like lunch," Beaufort laughed. He sounded like some villain from a James Bond movie.

"Give me a break, Beaufort," I said. "Four bases make up the rungs of the DNA ladder, adenine, guanine, cytosine, and thymine, make up the rungs of the DNA ladder. Each of those nucleic acids is a letter in the genetic alphabet, AGCT. AG are purines, TC pyrimidines."

"Yeah, Caddypod, tell him. We learned that in school. Right?"

Beaufort said: "Yes, CP. Let's see what level of knowledge you boys have of these things. Please, continue."

I continued: "The genetic alphabet, AGTC consists of four letters and ALL its words are three letters long."

"OK Mr. Doctor Smartyman. Tell me this, how many words does the genetic language have?" Beaufort asked.

I thought for a few moments. Finally I said: "four to the third, sixty four. Those sixty four letters make up words that specify amino acids to be generated in cell organelles. The rough and smooth endoplastic reticulum, to be used in protein synthesis." I had the old-or maybe not so old coot. He was a coot nonetheless.

"Well, well, well, CP. Very good. If you recall the word GCA specifies the synthesis of alanine. AAA, lysine, and so on. Some of those amino acids making up proteins could be specified by up to six or seven changes of words, some only by one. There used to be twenty amino acids."

"Used to be?" Grinder leaned forward.

"That's right. Until the Zeeneymen brothers tweaked the old human genome with a new nucleotide base. Yep, they came up with a new one, Mymine. That new nucleotide would be computer driven by what you used to call super computers and alter the translation process. You boys know the routine whereby the nucleic code is translated into the amino acids, then proteins now don't you?"

"Like the back of my hand," Grinder said.

I looked over at Grinder, who probably knew the back of his hand as no more than a place on his arm where his wrist watch needed to be. I just shook my head and looked back at Doc Beaufort.

"Those fellows used the new robotic aminatrons, that's what they called them, to fuss with the translator on the ribosome. Didn't matter what size Svedberg Unit was involved due to the fact that the super computers could calculate out to the billionth figure just where, when, and how, protein synthesis was headed. Yep, ready to go proteins were generated and incorporated wherever they needed to be to make the body work like a finely tuned machine. Yesiree, those computers could integrate those enhanced proteins into any part of the body at any moment automatically. Heck, the biochemical symphony was tuned to perfection and the mechanisms of proteins in action was like a grand orchestra. Diseases were put to rest for once and for all, staving off the funky angioneogenisis of cancer, tweaking cell division via mitosis, dyplasia...heck, the whole shebang. Cancer cells didn't have a chance and subverting the aging process came as an added benefit to boot. Pretty nifty, huh boys?"

"So you're sayin' there ain't no disease and there ain't no growin' old in the future?" Grinder narrowed his eyes in disbelief.

Our jaws were in our laps. We looked at each other and the room stood perfectly still. Just the sound of the nineteen fifties x-ray view box's neon light hummed and flickered like a thousand fireflies. Finally:

"Oh yes. When you passed through the scanner on into the waiting room, I got a snapshot of your genomes and transmitted the material to the lab, and sent back a tissue repair message just like that." He snapped his fingers. "Maybe that's why you should both be feelin' a little spry as well as...heh heh heh rejuvenated. Nothing like a strut through the old nanotechtonic rejuvinator."

"Hey, yous didn't go plantin' one of them extra nucleotides in us, didja?" Grinder stood up and started patting his sides. "I got enough already."

"Calm down now, Grinder, that's not such an easy task. The Zeeneyman innoculator's a bit more complicated than passin' through a simple nanotechtonic rejuvinator. Getting a mymine nuceotide base...that there is not something for everyone. Tossing in an extra nucleotide does not come cheap, nosiree. But let me tell you this. I'm about four, maybe five hundred years old." Beaufort smiled. "Don't tell the sheriff, but, he's about the same age and he's kind of particular about who and why folks like you show up unexpected in the cornfield. He's sort of like a sentinel for this particular time."

"Why you, why here, why this time, this era?" Grinder asked.

"Lots of questions boys." Doc Beaufort held up a palm and shook it. "Just take a breather and we'll get to these things."

"Yeah," Grinder continued, taking his seat, catching his breath only to let out a flurry of words. "Like this crap about portals, and how we got here, and why here, of all the freaking places in history, and those damned bodopidators or whatever you call them."

"Shut up, Grinder." I turned to Beaufort. "Let's get back to the harmonics..." I said, just as there was a knock at the door.

"Come in," Beaufort said.

It was Milly and another woman, as lovely as Milly was. This other woman also in nurses attire, she had something about her as striking as anything

I've ever seen. I didn't know what it was, but it didn't take long to feel it.

"Well, well, well, it looks like a fine meal is here for you boys. I see Milly's brought along another staff member. Say hello to CP and Grinder."

"Hello," she said, "my name is Nadine."

She was a tall, slender, beautiful, woman who when we locked eyes, I felt a jolt, like I'd been struck by lightning. It felt like an eternity until the fluttering of my heart slowed down and I could catch my breath. She was still holding my gaze. Her eyes were that sort of green that looked like it was out of an Emile Rousseau painting, from ocean to emerald to freaking Kryptonite. I felt like Clark Kent with a secret, but nobody I could share it with, but her. But we'd just met, never spoke and I was...in love? Too strange. I watched as she lay the plates on Doc Beaufort's desk, arrange the flatware and snap the cloth napkins in the air before placing them in our laps. Grinder was oblivious to all but the food. He'd had a fork and knife ready to dig in, and he did, within seconds. But this woman, I was dumbstruck...maybe it was the effects of that scanner. I felt like a teenager, or a puppy-maybe she just really turned me on. As she leaned over, the site of a perfectly shaped breast within a flesh colored brassiere had shown through what might have been a strategically unbuttoned nurses shirt.

The food was delicious. Grinder scarfed down his plate of eggs, gobbled up two slices of the buttery lathered toast before my first bite. The women looked on grinning in that way that waitresses do expecting a tip, but they were not waitresses and neither Grinder nor I had any currency that had yet to be minted, printed or mined. I waited until the ladies were either seated or left the room before chowing down. My mouth was watering but not so much as another sense struck a chord. Nadine, it was like I'd known her all my life, or I wanted to know her the rest of my life. I felt as if I'd been struck by lightning and despite all the craziness of the last twenty four to forty eight hours, hell the last decade of my life had evaporated and all I could feel beyond the initial frisson was a longing to spend my life with a woman who merely smiled at me. Maybe it was the scanner we passed through, the rejuvinator...what did he call it?"

"The nano technomic rejuvinator CP." Nadine said.

"You can read minds?" I said.

"Beaufort stood up, "we all can. Milly, you two skedaddle on down to the lab." Doc Beaufort pushed his wireless rimmed spectacles up his nose and grinned before saying, "of course they can read minds. We all can read minds that was one of many things that came out of those rotten cell phone wars. We have our own telepathic devices that run off our own cortical structures to communicate. Jeepers you fellas are from the darn stone age. How do you think we communicated after the cell phone wars and the epidemic of brain tumors?"

"I don't know. How am I supposed to know what happens in the future if I'm stuck in the past?" I said and thought how the hell does that work?

"The extra nucleotide base mymine, allows for the production of an amino acid of a protein that makes for intracellular matrix. This is not only structural but allows the nanotechnicians to install brain software like the Thinkreader. I think Amazon sells them real cheap these days, uh in the 2070s at least. Even with the el-cheapo version you can pick up whatever cortical buzz is going on in your own proximity. Those nanotech's do wonders boys, I've got one top of the line Thinkreader that let's me read thoughts across time and space and even interdimensionally. Then again the T.B.I., Time Bureau of Investigation foots the bill for it. The gals do too. Those are the rules if you wanna settle at some place in history for any period of time because they, the Feds, that is, want to keep track of you, make sure you don't break any laws like stock trades and that sort of thing. You know cashing in on outcomes you may already be aware of? F'rinstance you boys have only been here for a day or so. That ain't much, but early on there'd be folks comin' on back from a future making all sorts of ruckus with what they remembered of the future."

"Remembered of the future?" I was puzzled.

"Yes. Maybe I forgot to tell you that without the Zeeneyman Innoculator and mymine you start to forget what happened in the past, your past, that is. Sort of like having a mind full of vivid dreams when you wake up and they just float away as you get on with the day. Once you pass through a portal you can be a genius historian but after a spell you begin to forget everything you learned because those things didn't happen yet. The extra nucleotide and the Zeeneyman Innoculator prevents that from occurring."

"What the fuck's he talkin' about are you sayin' this guy can read my mind?." Grinder looked at me then over at Beaufort.

"I can only get a faint signal due to the fact that Grinder over there has a, hmm, let me say this gently...a weak cerebrocortical impulse. Sort of a garbled signal like these old time radio stations, you can't quite pick up the signal. Yes. That's what it sounds like, that rabble that you hear when somebody's flipping through the stations, all static and white noise and all."

"Is he sayin' I'm dumb CP?" Grinder stood up and posed as if to fight.

"I can pick up CP's thoughts just fine, Grinder." Beaufort replied in a cool even tone."

"What's that supposed to mean?" I said. Motioning for Grinder to chill out.

Beaufort continued: "Once that extra nucleotide's in the system thanks to the Zeeneyman Innoculator a body gets to regenerate itself. Yep, it's a fine thing. Oh, you're thinking can people regrow limbs and organs? Yes. But no you do not have the nucleotide base installed, at least not yet."

"How come you can pick up Caddypod's thoughts but not mine?"

"He's either a lot brighter than you or he's got some powerful thoughts. Think of what a top notch Thinkreader would do?"

"And that's expensive to install, right?" I said out loud.

"Yet," Grinder said looking up at Nadine. "does that mean you think we're gonna have some shit planted in us?

"It's the law boys, it's the law."

And with that, both Grinder and I passed out. The food must have been drugged and the last I heard was Beaufort's voice saying: "Go on girls, we have work to do here. Get them down to the lab. I have to get in touch with the T.B.I. and let them know that these fellas are here."

I didn't see anything, but when I awoke, Nadine was at my side. She said that the Sheriff had come into the office. Milly said that he stood in the door way for a few minutes sucking up the rejuvenating beam from the nanotechtonic rejuvinator, NTR, before saying: "I feel two hundred years younger." Then, "Where are those two bums?"

She went on to explain that Milly tried to hold him off but Sheriff Wilkens didn't want to hear of it. He said you and your friend were troublemakers in 2011 and that you were wanted. Beaufort's up there talking to him now.

Wait a second, I thought. Were we implanted with the additional cyclic nucleotide, mymine? We were able, to produce a new intracellular matrix which nanotechnologists could work with to install everything. From submucosal cells of the gut, to new appendages and organs, as well as devices, like the Thinkreader to communicate telepathically. I was looking at Nadine, who wasn't moving that luscious mouth and reading her thoughts. I better not look at her tits. But it was too late, she'd seen the wood rising in my groin area and blushed. Even twenty eighth century technology couldn't control nature's urges.

"It takes some getting used to the Thinkreader, but I must tell you, the T.B.I. insists you have a Trackmaster installed as well."

"What?"

"A Trackmaster keeps tabs on anyone and eveyone who's travelled through time, either accidentally or as part of a resettlement, like Beauf and Milly."

"What about you, Nadine?"

"I go from time to time to keep tabs on what people are doing."

You've got an awful lot of territory. I thought.

It was her turn to blush.

"I feel really good," I sat up supporting myself on my elbows."

"You should. You've been totally rejuvenated and every time you pass through a rejuvenating scanner your tissues will be realigned. Pretty cool isn't it CP?" She smiled. She had the sort of smile surrounded by the most kissable lips I've ever seen. And I did just that...

She didn't smack me, rather encouraged me and twenty minutes later we woke up Grinder. He wanted a drink or wasn't going to budge so Nadine fetched a Pabst Blue Ribbon faster than I could say my name ten times. He downed it even faster, saying: "America's Finest. I'll have another."

I considered not telling him about the mymine and the tracker but held off until he had a higher blood alcohol level. I knew that he would not enjoy having a tracker installed and I really didn't want to read his mind.

I looked at Nadine and replayed the outrageous sex we'd just had and blushed.

I guess Nadine read those thoughts because she blushed too and explained how I could tune those things out by pressing on parts of one of my eyebrows. Very cool, I thought to myself.

She just smiled. The door burst open. It was Doc Beaufort and one tall mean looking man in a light colored Stetson hat, aviator mirrored sunglasses, and a shit eating smile that showed off his large, dice cube shaped teeth. He was dressed in full trooper drag with all the trimmings of a fancy pants Gene Autry gone Nazi. He spoke in one nasty tone drawl heavy on the bass: "I am Sheriff Royal Wilkens, and you boys are in a heap of trouble." He had a hand on his sidearm.

HEAP OF TROUBLE

"Take it easy Roy," Doc Beaufort said. "They'll be just fine, leave them with me."

"No can do, Doc. They know too much."

"These boys are morons Royal. Let `em be."

"No can do, Beauf. I have a job to do. You boys are goin' to be havin' a bad day. A very bad day," and at that moment he drew his sidearm.

The Sheriff stared at Nadine, Grinder and his crumpled beer can, and me. He looked like he'd shoot us on the spot. His gun, a thirty eight special, from what I've seen of old cop movies was aimed at Grinder's gut.

"You boys ought not move a bit. You're not from around these parts, and passing through a portal puts you in violation of time travel rules, regulations, and transfers, subject to the authority of the T.B.I., which I am in charge of enforcing," he thumped his chest just above the tin badge. "You two are guilty of time traveling without a license." He said it in the way some petty tyrant with a little bit of authority does. Someone who makes the authority they have go as far as they can, even if it isn't much. But then again, he did have a gun.

Doc Beaufort stood behind him now. He was waving his hands to us, indicating that we comply. Just then Milly rushed in up from behind Doc Beafort, and thrust a shoulder into the Sheriff's right kidney.

"Milly!" Doc Beaufort hollered as he watched the Sheriff crumble to the ground, his gun scattering across the Linoleum. Beaufort motioned for us to get out the door. Judging by his rapid hand motions he meant but quick. He feigned sympathy for the fallen lawman, "Sheriff are you all right?"

Nadine, Grinder and I rushed out through the waiting room, pausing a few moments each in the beam emitted by the nanotechtonic rejuvinator.

"Oh those NTR rays feel so good," Nadine said, doing a full Veronica with the sweater she'd taken from her shoulders. "Go ahead CP, you've got to recharge yourself, who knows how long it will be until the next time we get to rejuvenate.

"What the fuck's she talkin' about CP?" Grinder said.

I twirled around a few times and yanked Grinder into the scanner. "Just do what I did," I said just as the sounds of footsteps and cursing rang out in the distance.

I grabbed one of the chairs from the waiting room and shut the office door hard, smashed the chair in the hallway and jammed the pieces under the door. It wouldn't hold back an army but, looking down at my handy work, the gun in my hand, we could at least stall off John Q. Law long enough to make a getaway. At that moment there was a bang at the door. The Sheriff was on our tails, shouting that he was going to get our sorry asses and make sure we never get out of jail. Nadine grabbed my arm just above the elbow and tugged. She tilted her chin toward the door to the chiropodists office across the hall. Grinder looked at me, then Nadine and the three of us barged into the suite. We were all short of breath and terrified. Why had Nadine joined us? Why did Beaufort and Milly help us escape? Why was the Sheriff so intent on enforcing our being there?

"You'll find out soon enough," Nadine said.

"What's she talkin' about, CP?" Grinder said, pinching his temples as if he had brain freeze from sucking down a slurpee too fast. "Shit, am I reading your minds, CP, Nadine?"

"Yeah. You can read minds Grinder, so can she, and so can I, so stop looking at her tits and thinking about another beer and concentrate on how the fuck we're going to get out of this fine mess."

And just like that, I realized we were in the presence of a hunched over man in his mid fifties, maybe sixties with wire rimmed glasses, a shiny bald spot in the center of a salt and pepper crop of hair, cut in a fashion similar to Moe from the Three Stooges. He dug his hand into his gray smock with patch like pockets, and grinned like a spider who'd just had a few flies get stuck in its web. He looked us up and down, sizing us up as if we were paying a visit to the old chiropodist.

"Well, we don't ordinarily accept clients without an appointment but you three seem like you have some problems. My secretary's off today but I can start the whirlpool for the lady. Hehehe," he giggled like some wacked out hunchback from a horror movie in black and white. But this was some living color shit and smelled like Desenex, foot powder, and stinky feet.

"Fill out these papers," he said shuffling over to a file cabinet." He walked as if he either had horrible hemorrhoids or there were pebbles in his shoes, handed us some forms and hobbled away. He actually hobbled as if his hunchback was a weight he couldn't get out from under. "Any of you care for a Chesterfield? Best there is, Doctor recommended too..." He removed a pack and tapped out a cigarette, placed it between his lips and motioned the three of us into the inner treatment room of his chiropody office with a craggily pale finger.

We were in an examination room of sorts illuminated from the huge window facing what I later came to know as Main Street.

"Dr. Herman Duss, that's what they call me. Why don't you take a seat young lady, please," the hunchbacked chiropodist said. A regular Quasimodo.

"It smells nice," she had a puzzled look on her face yet acquiesced, knowing that there was trouble in the hallway and the coast might not yet be clear. She'd clearly read the hunchback's mind because I caught her blush and straigten out her skirt, flattening it down so he couldn't see her frilly pink panties. I'd already seen them and doubted if she was apt to share this with her new foot doctor. He was readying his paraphanalia on a tray beside the table like some crazed, diabolical wizard about to cast a spell. He turned to Grinder and me, and said proudly: "That's genuine Naugahyde folks," he slapped the arm of the chair proudly. "Top of the line."

I watched the cigarette dangling between his lips as he spoke and motioned for Nadine to relax by holding my palm face down and worked it like a yo yo as I took in the sights. The chair, jeez, the thing looked like an ornate dental chair, faux gold trim impregnated with colored beads shaped like feet. The smell of fake leather fit in well with the motif of the sole treatment room separated by flimsy curtains which hid the swirling foot bath. The hum of water sloshing around got my attention and Duss must have caught my glance.

"That's the whirlpool warmin' up young fella," he said torching up his Chesterfield with a Zippo and inhaling deeply as Nadine appeared to relax in the chair and rested the backs of her ankles on the little platform that had a tray of sorts, probably to collect callus, corn and nail shavings. Duss looked at Nadine, inspected her uniform, pursed his lips, letting the lower lip jut out a bit before taking another drag and saying: "You must be a nurse young lady?" He was looking at her feet. "You might want to take off your shoes."

"What are you some sort of clown? Of course she's a fucking nurse you retard! No wonder you're a fucking chiropodist...Shit, they're gonna call you guys PODIATRISTS, you know what that is?" Grinder had his fists all balled up planted on his hips. "What the fuck's the matter with you, haven't you ever heard of podiatric medicine? Dammit, I've studied with podiatrists, they're physicians, and what you're doing is out of the stone age!"

"Excuse my friend," I grabbed Grinder by the scruff of his neck and pulled him to the other side of the curtain. With the buzz of the whirlpool loud enough to drown out my words. "Grinder, you asshole, this is nineteen fifty eight and the word podiatry hasn't even been entered into the English language let alone podiatric medicine. Shit, you sound like a lunatic to this poor schmuck. Get a grip, man or you'll piss the guy off and we'll end up dealing with John Q. We gotta hole up here at least until we put together a plan."

"You're right, CP. I got carried away. I need a drink, you think this guy has a liquor cabinet?"

"I looked around the shadowy room. There were wooden filing cabinets and shelves filled with books, bottles, and all sorts of ancient-well not really ancient from the old chiropodist, Dr. Duss's point of view, but to us...some really old shit.

Just then the curtain parted. It was Duss, staring at us, shaking his head.

"Are you boys all right?" Duss said. His voice was attuned to the sounds of his whirlpool and was able to speak a few octaves above the whirling and whooshing.

"We're fine. My friend here's just a little shaken from the ride over. "You wouldn't happen to have an alcoholic beverage, would you?" I said, winking at Grinder to which I whispered: "I don't know if chiropodists could prescribe drugs in the fifties so maybe he keeps a bottle stashed-shit, I would if I had to do the crap he's doing."

Duss poked his head through the curtain. "The young nurse has a mighty thick HD 5 that needs some work. Might take me a spell, but yes, I do have an office bottle over there on the shelf. He pointed his double chin toward the file cabinets, walked over to it and pulled out a bottle of Early Times Rye Whisky and handed it to me.

"I have a couple of glasses over in the john. Help yourselves. When I'm finished maybe you can explain to me just what the heck you meant by puddy ack rick medicine. If you boys need a doctor doctor Doc Beaufort's across the hall and Jim Collins is the dentist next door. You best settle down and we'll chat in a spell."

I handed the bottle to Grinder and he thanked the chiropodist and said: "Ayche Dee Five?" It sounded like he spit it out.

"Son, that's complicated medical jargon for a hyperkeratotic buildup at the level of the interphalangeal joint on the lateral, or the outside portion of the fifth toe. It's going to take some serious paring down to give the lovely Nurse Nadine some relief." He turned and parted the curtain to take a seat on the stool at the foot of the fake diamond encrusted chiropody chair.

Grinder yanked out the cork and took a slug. I just shook my head and pulled the bottle away from him and said: "manners, Grinder-behave yourself. Besides, I could use a drink myself." And pointed toward where the bathroom might be.

He pivoted and went toward the head to grab some glasses.

I sat down next to the old chiropodist and watched him trim the thick skin on Nadine's toe. She looked over at me and smiled. I could read her thoughts and she could read mine. I got to thinking about Doc Beaufort's rant regarding the future. The fact that I had a new cyclic nucleotide and pondered the notion that I could very well live a long life, of course I could still get shot. I was pretty much conversing with her telepathically, here's how it went:

At some point scientists added a new cyclic nucleotide, mymine, to the essential four nucleotide bases, adenine, thymine, guanine, and cytosine, which any set of the three made up the rungs of the DNA ladder.

By using nanotechnology, they created a mechanical plasma sort of thing the size of a molecule and added it, mymine, to the mix of AGTC. Was it a purine, like adenine and guanine? Or a pyrimidine like thymine and cytosine?

Neither, it is a unique bioelectroplasmic structure which is introduced into the human body and is self replicated by way of an immunologic response. Once introduced into the human body, the inflammatory process is set into play and the mymine nanochip becomes a substrate which is converted by dehydrogenases-removing several hydrogen atoms-activating the nitrogen based structure which is incorporated into the intracellular matrices. I heard her thoughts and looked at her and nodded for her to continue.

This man made substance in turn goes into the pool of bioavailable substances collected in the production of deoxyribonucleic acid and we have triplets containing a nucleotide, mymine, which we can control via super computing to integrate into the rungs of the DNA ladder, just as GCA specifies the synthesis of the amino acid, alanine, GCM specifies the synthesis of the amino acid, not previously known as DYALININE in both L and D isomers which become racemic in an aqueous solution, the blood at optimal pH of 7.2-7.6. The DYALAMINE is largely unrecognized by the immune system and is treated as a foreign body, but not before it is incorporated into a long chain protein of OUR-the supercomputer's-choice. This is done so by way of controlling the body's intricate biochemical reactions in a manner which can incorporate mymine implanted proteins of ANY sort to ANY location of the body through a cascade of chemical events ranging from simple tissue repair, and consequent scar formation, to complex pathways ranging from the nitric oxide cycle to inborn genetic anomalies like Huntingtons disease. The aotosomal recessive traits can be modified by having mymine incorporated into the sequencing issues inherent to the disease. Huntingtons has an abundance of CAG, CAG, CAG, sequencing, once we introduce our own computer directed M, we can interfere with the sequencing itself, but that's just the start of what's been done. By adding M to structural proteins, like the trabecula of bone, connective tissues of muscles, tendons, ligaments and skin, regenerative submucosal cells in the gut smooth muscle of the heart and blood vessels and the nervous tissues. We can not only replace damaged and or aging tissues, but regenerate tissues and guide specific enzymes and structural proteins to deliver a decisive punch to the destruction of ANY disease-including the elimination of ALL human cancers. This became the template to veritably create an immortality.

As long as the computer isn't fucked around with, that guides the cells. I thought.

The computers are in orbit. Satellites were sent off in the mid twenty fifth century to automatically detect, repair, and maintain, the mymine of all of those implanted.

People can live forever, provided there isn't some drastic shift in the earth.

"Like a shift in alkalinity or acidity for any sustained period of time?" I said aloud.

Nadine spoke too: "That's why the first disease we eliminated was diabetes and its ketoacidosis. Gotcha CP. There's an eternity waiting for you."

"But not everyone is ready for this..." I said.

Herman Duss, Doctor of Surgical Chiropody stopped what he was doing and looked up. "What the heck are you two talking about?"

Nadine looked at him and said: "It's just an inside thing."

"Hmmm," the old chiropodist murmured and went back to paring down the dead skin over her pinky toe.

A heavy silence fell among us, and the whirlpool hummed gently from the room where Grinder sat behind a curtain pounding down Rye

Whiskey. Nadine had told Dr. Duss despite his insistence that she didn't want to put her feet in the filthy looking hot tub knowing she may have to leave in a hurry. I agreed. I settled into alternating my staring at Nadine and gazing out the window at Main Street on this fine May morning in nineteen fifty eight. I marvelled at how tranquil they both looked, and considered the notion that this was a simpler time in human history, sometimes regarded as the Good old Days and smirked, shaking my head at the thoughts.

My reverie was interrupted by a loud crash. I looked at Nadine, then Duss, and we froze staring tentatively at each other. Then we heard shattering glass and Grinder's voice broke the silence. He stood there, eyes bulging, nostrils flared, his face flushed.

"We gotta split, man. They're out there in the waiting room, the Sheriff and the Deputy too. I heard them, they're talking about taking us out and shooting us!"

"Deputy Jerry Barns? That gentle soul wanting to shoot us? What did they think we were, space invaders?"

Nadine looked over at me and said: "Yes," as she got out of the chiropody chair. Duss slid the stool toward the window and was gazing out.

"I don't know who you people are, but the damn Army is out there and they've broken out some heavy weapons. Just who the hell are you?" The old chiropodist asked.

"I'm a physician from the future," Grinder thumped his chest in the way people who've had one too many drinks do and missed, hitting his upper arm instead.

"What the hell is that?" Duss asked.

He looked frightened, but I didn't think he'd rat us out, especially when I considered the fact that the gun I'd snatched off the floor, the one that belonged to the Sheriff was pointed right at him. Shit I hated guns and I sure as hell wasn't going to shoot the old guy. But there were people in the lobby, people who didn't mean us well. No, not at all.

Nadine put her hand on my forearm pushing the weapon down. "Listen Dr. Duss, as hard as it might be to believe, we're not from around here," she motioned with her chin to the window then the waiting room which was starting to sound like some serious activity had begun and said: "If you help us, we'll help you," she took a small sack out of her nurses smock and tossed it on the floor. A few diamonds spilled out.

"Is there another way out of here?" she asked.

"Is that stuff stolen?" Duss said. "Are you thieves? Is that what all the ruckus is about?"

"No, I said," the gun was back in the waistband of my nineteen fifty eight jeans at the small of my back. "We're time travelers. We're from the future." I said it and wondered just how ridiculous it sounded.

"Time travelers?" Duss looked at the stones and shrugged. "Don't got much use for fake diamonds, but the future? You say you're from the future? Can you tell me about it?"

Grinder butted in: "You hear that shit in the lobby and that mob out there on the street? What makes you think we have time to stop and chat old man?"

"Grinder," I said. "Chill. The guy's freaked out."

"I know a way out of here where no one can know the better. I'll show you if you take me with you and tell me about the future."

"Why? There's no future for chiropody-you'll be a relic." Grinder said matter of factly.

"I'm a relic now and that damned Sheriff, Royal Wilkens he calls himself, he's been a thorn in my backside for years. He's a son of a bitch and comes around here like he runs Sherwood Forest."

The Sheriff of Nothingham, a petty tyranical putz who'd wanted to keep time straight was getting on my nerves. Why the fuck didn't he just bug off? I thought.

Nadine had read my thoughts and replied telepathically: He is making sure there are no changes in the space-time continuum, and can not allow any interruptions or a change in the past will alter his future. He has been here for years making sure that your arrival would go just so.

He knew we were coming.

As sure as the sun comes up. The only possible outcome for him is to keep both of you here and make sure that Beaufort and Milly remain just as they are.

But what about you, Nadine?

I'm here to take you and that jerk Grinder to another time to change the future. If I fail, I'll cease to exist.

So we can't take the old chiropodist?

"No. Dr. Duss, we cannot take you to the future. But if you help us out of here I will give you information that will change your life and that of all the generations that follow."

"Like what?" Duss said.

"Like how to do a few procedures and stop hunching over a chair shaving corns." Grinder said. "And you Nadine I didn't appreciate you thinking that I was a jerk. I can read minds too you know..."

"He's right and he's wrong, Duss," Nadine said. "I can tell you about what will happen in the next five years and the rest is up to you. We'll start with a few stock market tips, some natural disasters and sporting events. You can bet as you will but if I were an investor I would buy as much stock in this list of companies and hold on to them," she grabbed a slip of paper and wrote furiously. Finally she looked up and stared at Grinder. "You are a jerk and you only have a weak pickup signal for thoughts. You weren't originally part of the plan, but since you're here, I'm stuck with you."

The old chiropodist took the slip of paper. "You sure about this stuff?"

I looked at the paper and said: "You'll be a multimillionaire in three years. In the mean time go to Detroit and do this," I grabbed a number ten blade and dipped it in a glass bead sterilizer and held it up. "Next time someone has an H D 5 poke a hole in the skin and cut the tendon, right here on top and down on the bottom of the toe and take a rasp..." I took a small file and made a motion of sorts, "And file the bone down. You can do these things in Michigan they have chiropodists doing surgery there. They can write prescriptions and give injections. This town is a freak zone and if you want to make it you'll get as far away from here as you can."

"Doc Beaufort will give you all the details you need and help you with what's going to happen."

The door crashed open. Duss looked like he'd seen his own death, and ushered us back behind the curtain. There he herded us toward the bookshelf, he yanked open a file cabinet and one of the shelves slid open. "Come on," he said. "Come with me," he motioned for us into the dark chamber.

"This better not be some kinda setup old man," Grinder said.

"Shut the fuck up," I said and pushed him into the cubby behind the shelves.

We followed him down a corridor behind the wall, and felt our way along a dark hallway. Was it a trap? I didn't know but the sounds of shuffling feet and shouting came from the room just as the bookshelf secret door snapped shut.

"Shhh..." Duss had a finger to his lips. "This leads to the back alley."

"Shit they got the friggin' troops out, you don't think they got the alley covered? Shit, CP, this is bullshit, we're fucked, totally fucked."

"Grinder, or whatever you're name is, shut up," Duss said. "This hall leads to another building. I had it set up so the colored people who come to get their corns scraped wouldn't get harassed by the Sheriff. You know how it is for colored folks these days."

"Duss," I said. "In 2008 the president of the United States is a Negro. And black people are not called Negroes anymore, they're called African Americans."

"Well, I'll be darned," the old chiropodist said just as we reached a staircase and began our descent.

"Hey Duss, take every penny you have and buy as much Coca Cola as you can. Trust me on this. Hold on to it. Five thousand dollars invested in Coca Cola today will be one hundred thousand dollars in nineteen seventy two. And even though Nixon, Dwight's VP loses to JFK he gets shot and his VP, LBJ takes over and the Vietnam war heats up, don't worry about it. The Russians will end up our allies and the bad guys will be a whole new gang of bad guys..."

"CP," Nadine said firmly. "That's enough. I wrote down all he needs to know."

"Come with me folks," Duss led us to a nineteen fifty seven Chevrolet parked in an alley nearly a block away from the office. We loaded in and he started the engine.

"Where to folks?"

"Take us out of the city limits, toward the cornfields," Nadine said.

I watched from the rear window of Herman Duss' Chevy the troop trucks, two, maybe three Sherman Tanks, their turrets aimed toward the second floor above the hardware store and dress shop.

There were soldiers populating a perimeter around the front of the building and what looked like a high ranking officer in a Jeep with a long antenna suggesting a radio of sorts. The soldiers moved about cautiously, their weapons readied. There was a patrol car which had driven on up over the curb. The driver's side door was open and a soldier was stationed there with his rifle aimed at the entrance.

No one seemed to notice the Chevy which was well beyond the perimeter. I lowered myself into the backseat. Duss draped his arm across the bench seat and turned his head, and glanced at Nadine, Grinder, and me, crouching as we drove toward the outskirts of town.

Maybe we'd get to the cornfield and jolt toward who knows where. At this point I had no idea but Nadine's thoughts were reassuring. Everything was going to be OK as long as we made it to the field of corns. She knew what had to be done.

I was beginning to settle into a quiet reverie when Duss hit the brakes thrusting the three of us forward.

"Darn it, we've got trouble," he said.

"What is it?" Grinder said. "A road block?"

Shit, I thought. Just what we needed. I could see some jerkoff interrogating us, threatening prison time...Who would believe we were time travelers? Shit shit shit.

Somehow we made it and left Duss sweating behind the wheel of his Chevy, a cigarette dangling from his lower lip.

"This is where you travel through time and space. is there some kind of machine?" Duss asked anxiously.

"No," Nadine said. "Just sit there and rev the engine of your car. Put a foot on the brake, put the vehicle, in neutral and bring it up to this sound and hold it..." She opened her mouth and let out a wail. She motioned for me and grinder to get out of the car and head into the cornfield. Duss was doing as she said and when his car's engine matched the chords coming from her larynx she stopped. "Now keep that up until you can't do it any longer. Maybe five minutes. And use the material we've jotted down."

"Thank you," he said," and held the accelerator in place and watched us disappear into the cornfield. There was no path so we just swatted the stalks aside and forged into the dense jungle of unshucked niblets.

We trudged maybe a hundred yards when Nadine took an odd looking plastic object from a pocket of her nurses smock. She held it up, smiled, and said:

"Flutaphone, boys. A flutaphone." She tilted her head to the side. "Hear that," she nudged her chin.

We looked toward Duss' Chevy maintaining a regular rate and rhythm. She raised the flutaphone and began to blow. An eerie tone, a song of sorts and it went on like that for a spell, seemed like hours but it was just seconds until things started to get odd. Grinder looked at me, shrugged and pointed up at the sky. Clouds had gathered. The stalks of corn had begun swaying as the wind kicked up and the sky grew even darker. The combined sounds seemed to permeate the space we occupied, our arms, at least mine, felt heavier, it was as if gravity had changed. And then I watched lightning dance from one dark cloud to another, and a sudden crack, then another, and just like that, there was a blur, a mass of mirror-like space which opened in the space between us.

"That's the portal," Nadine put down her flutaphone. "We have to move fast." She said, motioning us to jump into the blurry mass. "It'll only remain open for a few seconds."

Was there another side to the shimmering mirror we'd, leapt though? Or were we jumping through air? I was suddenly exhausted, yet oddly exhilarated. We were still in a cornfield but was it the same cornfield? I looked at Nadine, then Grinder and stood there as the portal disappeared just as mysteriously as it had appeared. Nadine wore an expression as if it were no big deal, but Grinder appeared freaked out. His skin was ashen, hair disheveled, more so than usual. I could see myself in my mind and looked pretty shitty to myself. But gauging my appearance by the gaze of Nadine I must have looked just fine. We stood there in silence for what might have been hours but I knew it was only a minute or so. The silence was broken by the sound of something in the sky, a slow high pitched wind then, a steady sound, like... a jet plane, an airliner. I looked up and saw the vapor trail of a Boeing 727. I knew we were not in 1958 and stared at the jet against a cloudless afternoon sky. It was up there, along with a few criss crossing jet trails in various states of dispersion at several thousands of feet up. I could make out one thing for certain and that was the markings identifying the carrier, Eastern Airlines. I knew we were not home in the twenty first century because Eastern had ceased to be a commercial airline in 1991.

SOME OTHER TIME

I looked at Nadine and said: "This ain't the fifties, and with all that airline traffic there must be an airport nearby."

I knew that there was an airport somewhere near Hoogerstown. The place that hadn't been built back in 1958 on account they hadn't completed the dam that made Lake Hooger. This made for the plot of land, developers set to build up in the late sixties and early seventies. I remember how it was touted as the "Town of Tomorrow" Hoogerstown, and the upscale "Hooger Springs" the small town, big city, for the well heeled family. It turned into a ramshackle crime ridden ghetto in the nineties, and a flat out dump in the double otts. The airport was retired and left to decay to the point where weeds grew out from the cracks in the runway. Yeah we travelled in time. But this didn't seem like the time I hoped for. "Do you have any clue as to what year we're in?" I asked.

She shrugged her shoulders."

"If we're in a different time then let's get the hell out of this field, ain't gonna be nobody lookin' for us." Grinder said sharply.

"No, Grinder. They're either dead, retired or both." I said mainly to shut him up.

Nadine started walking in the direction we entered the cornfield in just moments earlier. I felt odd that so many years passed in just a few minutes. But hey, that's time travel.

When we poked our heads out from the corn stalks the first thing that caught my eyes was the road. What was a two lane highway was now four. There were cars, more modern cars traveling at high speeds running back and forth, passing each other and honking their horns. There were headrests in the cars that meant it must be somewhere... when were they mandated the late sixties early seventies?

We had begun walking toward the town. It looked different, very different. I could see the Golden Arches and the array of advertisements which hadn't been there earlier.

"We should check in at the office," Nadine said.

The little town had become a dumpier, more commercialized version of when we'd left. There was a newspaper box, the date May 6, 1978. There was a picture of the President, Jimmy Carter and the headlines about some Peace Process in the Middle East, Begin and Sadat were set to chat. They were voting for a new Pope and Jimmy Connors was set to play Bjorn Borg at Wimbledon. On our way down Main Street the roads had pot holes and were crowded with people on their lunch break. They were decked out in polyester. Mustachioed men in leisure suits, women in Farrah Faucet hair styles strutting bralessly smoking Virginia Slims. The nifty Camaros and Firebirds radio's pulsed out disco music. The occasional Hotel California wafted out of a car with a bumper sticker extolling a hatred for disco and the thick aroma of cannabis filled the air. The traffic lights were as up to date as nineteen seventy eight was ready for.

The movie theatre had undergone some changes and the marquee read that the Deer Hunter was playing, and some posters for Midnight Express, Coming Home, and Heaven Can Wait, reflected how far cinematography had come in twenty years. Cat on a Hot Tine Roof had been considered a classic by now, and every home had a color TV. We knew this for sure because the old mom and pop hardware store was now an electronics store selling hi fi's, color TV's, and the Mr. Coffee machines...damn people were standing in line.

We caught an occasional glance, grimace, and stare, from passerbys what with our flannel shirts and jeans and Nadine wearing her late fifties edition of nursing attire. But nobody seemed to care as they went to and fro on their way to wherever it was they were hustling. I could almost hear the Chicago song: "Doesn't Anybody Really Know What Time it is?" When Nadine tugged my upper arm and rushed me across the street. Grinder followed, taking in the sites of the richly oozing days of feminism and was thinking out loud. I'll spare noting his meanderings.

There was a pharmacy at the corner where the market had been. It was part of a chain and what had once been a small park had become a parking lot. There were some apartment buildings several stories tall, and office buildings as well. The Norman Rockwellish town sort of reflected the death of the artist in its hither nither, helter skelter growth, and general insouciance of the culture. A busy caffeine and nicotine driven bustle of a world not yet computerized had very much engaged in self absorption.

Grinder asked: "Ya think I could pick up a pack of smokes? Maybe a pinto?" He was staring at a clump of shadowy structures across the street. A liquor store with an adjoining bar, and what looked like an X-rated bookstore. There was an alley next to the oasis that looked like the sort of place you wouldn't want to get stuck in.

"Hey you guys," Grinder said. "Looks like a decent watering hole." He was adjusting his gold chains and inspecting his pinky ring, holding his hand out in approval.

"Looks like a dump, Grinder. Do you have anything that remotely looks like money?" I asked.

Grinder had already begun crossing the street.

"Hold on Grinder," I said, as Nadine and I followed him toward the boozery. There was a man who'd come out of the alley next to the seedy bar next door and despite our objections Grinder forged on.

"Yeah," Grinder said, making a beeline to the liquor store smiling, "I got me some loot."

He had his hand on the door handle. The plate glass on the front window was plastered with discounts on beer, Marlboro, Newport, and Kool cigarettes. Grinder yanked it open and bells rang, as if Rudolph the Reindeer just got kicked in the balls.

Grinder paused for a moment looking at us, motioning with one hand to follow when a man who must have been lurking in the alley next to the liquor store revealed himself and tapped Grinder on the shoulder. He stopped again and looked over toward us, then at the stranger, and we heard:

"Yo, what it is?" The voice of the man had a sing-song quality and deep bass timbre that sounded like it came from the bottom of an oil drum.

Nadine and I were already on the sidewalk as Grinder held up a palm to the man and said: "Hold that thought," and entered the store.

"Thass cool dude," oil can man said.

I looked at the black guy. He was wearing an Afro style haircut puffed out from beneath his Fedora with a large brightly colored feather in it. He was smoking a long thin brown cigarette and wore a trim leather jacket, spread collar shirt, and had a big medallion dangling on a thin chain over his dark skinned chest. He had on sunglasses, bell bottom pants, and as Grinder came out of the store the Negro looked at Grinder.

Grinder stood there with his brown paper sack and stared at the man and said: "Whazzup my man?"

I heard the spread collar hipster say to Grinder: "Say what, Jim? I ain't your, man," he flicked his cigarette so hard, sparks flew across the street. He pivoted to face my friend. Shit.

"What's happenin'?" Grinder had already opened his liquor bottle, took a swig and was fiddling with his fresh pack of Winstons. "Have a pop, relax," he said in a manner which diffused any situation his idiocy may have sparked.

Nadine and I were about five steps away from the two men and we heard the guy speak to Grinder, he said:

"Yo man, you want some blow maybe a little action?" He made the universal breast sign-that's when someone takes the palms of their hands and lays them flat against their upper torso, cups their hands and pulls them out.

"Nice tits, dude..."

"I could dig some of that action..." Grinder said placing a cigarette in his mouth and glancing over at me and Nadine.

"Grinder," I said harshly narrowing my eyes and shaking my head at the afro man in shades. He held up his hands in a thass cool demeanor as we stood in front of the liquor store. A day drinker exited the adjacent bar, glanced at the four of us and hurried away.

"CP, I don't think we should interact with these people until we've checked in with Doc Beaufort." Nadine said as we stood there.

"These people?" The afro man put his hands on his hips and looked at Nadine like a bug needing to be squashed, and tilted his head down to look over his aviators. He spoke in an adversarial, threatening tone: "Who you callin' these people?"

Grinder had already finished lighting up his smoke and took another swig from the pint of hooch when I intervened, hoping to diffuse the situation. The liquor store clerk witnessed what may have been a confrontation and came to the front door and poked his head out. He was a short Oriental man in his forties or so and said: "Go way take your business someplace else," and left the door open. "Go. No make a scene here I got a store to run. You no buy you go."

"Just be cool. We ain't from around here brother, this ain't no African American thing we're just new in town." Grinder said in that flippant man of the street tone. That worked well enough in the twenty first century that Grinder managed to keep most of his teeth.

If you knew Grinder that would have been surprising. But in nineteen seventy eight, calling an African American an African American didn't quite make any sense coming out of the mouth of a white guy dressed in full farming attire. The liquor store clerk looked edgy as the black man spoke angrily.

"Say what, Jim?" The afro pick that was stuck in his hair was now in the coke dealers hand. "I oughta put your mo fo eye out fo dat kinda talk, callin' me a Affero...Whazzat s'posed to mean?" He had the hair tending weapon readied to thrust toward Grinder's face when a patrol car, a black and white pulled up. There was a short burst of the siren and afro man ducked against the concrete wall adjacent to the bar.

A few beats went by as we stood there frozen. Finally after what seemed like an eternity we heard a voice ring out. "Don't move."

It was a man's voice amplified through a squeaky megaphone. There was something familiar in the tone and pitch despite the feedback. I sensed It was that of a person I'd heard at some other time, some other place. With our backs turned away from the squad car I couldn't quite tell for sure if it was any policeman I might know. I turned to face him. There was something painfully familiar about him, I squinted and nudged Grinder. "Does that guy look familiar?" I asked.

The law man was out of the car and on the sidewalk before we could jump, his gun drawn and he hadn't aged a bit, not one bit at all in twenty years. "Now I got you." He smiled, and those big dice cube teeth glistened in the mid day sun.

We dove toward the boozery and the liquor store clerk was standing there with a shotgun aimed in our general direction. Just as he took aim the three of us dashed toward the bar's entrance, joining afro man.

"Shit," I said to him. "We're in a fucking cross fire."

"I'm gettin' my ass outta here motherfuckers. I don't want no trouble. Shit, damn honkies!" He pushed off and disappeared into an alley.

Two gun shots in rapid progression rang out from the general direction of the liquor store. The law man ducked, dove, and took cover, behind the open door of his squad car. The three of us scattered and after a long silence we heard Sheriff Royal Wilkens speaking through his cackling megaphone.

"Come out with your hands up. All of you!" He scurried for cover behind the black and white. "Lower your weapon, backup is on the way."

There was another gunshot that hit the squad car, shattering the police car's back seat passenger window.

"Hop Sing, put the damn gun away. I have this under control, dammit." Wilkens said. "You owe me a window. Now put the damn gun away and go back into the store."

During their brief exchange, I pushed away from the wall, grabbed Nadine and motioned Grinder to make a run for it. Afro clearly knew the hood. "Follow the schvartza!" I yelled, "that dude's gotta know these streets."

"He ain't no bopeep, CP," Grinder said.

"No shit, let's bust a move," I shouted to Nadine and Grinder as we ducked into the alley where afro oozed into.

"Stop or I'll shoot you from behind," Wilkens shouted. I saw him holding his gun in the air. He fired a warning shot. I looked over my shoulder, his sidearm was pointed in our general direction. A heard something sizzle past my left ear and then the burst of gunfire. The bullet hit one of the walls in the alley and ricocheted off.

At that, I grabbed both Nadine and Grinder and hurled them out of the line of fire, we were behind a dumpster.

I was in a crouched position next to a huge metal dumpster. Grinder was huddled a few feet away, his back flush with the wall of the alley next to the building we'd just left. He took a quick nip from his liquor bottle and gave us a wave. Nadine nudged my arm and pointed with her chin to the liquor store. The store's clerk joined the Sheriff and they exchanged words. An eternity seemed to have passed as they spoke. Finally they began a slow steady march toward us.

Nadine, Grinder, and I, thrust back out into the alley and sprinted to the next dumpster where afro man was catching his breath. "Do you know a way outta here?" I said.

"Maybe, but I don't usually needs no company," he said, a sour look on his face.

"Yeah, well there might be something in it for you brother," Grinder, man of the street said.

"I ain't your brother motherfucker, but I do like them gold chains," he said staring at Grinder's jewelry.

"Hey this is the real deal man." I said.

"Yeah? So's them guns." The black man said.

"He'll give you some gold if you can get us out of here," I said. Giving Grinder a bulging eye stare that said: If you don't give the guy the fucking chains I'll rip them off your fucking neck, asshole. Thanks to the telepathy Nadine shot him a telepathic burst of agreement and the chains came off just as another shot rang out.

"Less do it " afro man said, and we joined up with the pimp and broken into a run cutting into another alley. This one was dark with huge trash containers brimming with garbage on either side.

"I don't know who you people is but we got the heat on us. You come up with more booty?" It wasn't a question as much as it was an offer, command and a threat.

Just as he finished his sentence another burst came out of the megaphone: "Stop and put your hands up or I will be forced to shoot to kill. Those last shots were just to get your attention."

I would later recall that shooting us in nineteen seventy eight would prevent us from reaching the twenty first century, and being transported back to 1958. The portals and nanotech chips implanted in us by Doc Beaufort would NOT cause a rift in the space-time continuum. This would make life easier for the T.B.I., the agency, that Wilkens allegedly worked for. But wouldn't the mymine chips help rejuvenate us if we got shot? Nadine must have sent a fast and hard telepathic burst because the word "NO" echoed in my cranial cavity.

"We're from the future," I said hastily. "If that guy catches up with us, we're all dead."

"What the fu...?" Aviator man in leather said. "I don't know who you is, but I got enough blow on me that if we gets busted I be lookin' at a dime at the big house motherfucker. I gots my car over there." He stopped, pivoted, and yanked open a door behind one of the trash containers. "You motherfuckers better be cool or I gonna keel you dead mah sef. And I ain't forgot about the gold. I gonna truss you people juss because you needs me and anybody on the run from that crazy ass police man muss be OK, `sides, dead folks don't pay no bills and them gems wouldn't do me no good in no evidence bin. By the way people call me Chalk. Dig it?"

Grinder looked at him and said: "Chalk?"

Chalk said: "You gotsa a prollem wit dat honkey? I bees like chalk cause I get rubbed the wrong way I dissapears. Dig it?"

"We dig it" I said, "Let's just get the fuck out of here."

The door was largely invisible and where it led was as confusing to me as it was to Nadine and Grinder. But our choices weren't like Alice, who could've elected NOT to have followed the rabbit down the hole. After all no one was shooting at her. I shrugged, as did my time travelling colleagues and we followed afro man into a dark vast high ceiling space. An old warehouse I suspected. There were small windows way up above and a labyrinth of pipes, steel cross beams, and catwalks, in various states of decay, disrepair, and dilapidation, dangled dubiously above. There were boxes, crates, and containers, scattered about. Chalk led us toward a glass windowed cubby, an office of sorts, where a woman sat behind a desk. She was an African American woman in her early thirties or so and an IBM Selectric typewriter was on the desk. She looked at Chalk, Nadine, Grinder, and me, and put an unlit Newport in her mouth, and notched her head toward Chalk.

"Who they?" She asked.

"They cool, Tamina," Chalk said as he lit the cigarette.

"The Man be on their asses. Seems these honkey white folks is undesirables-and that make `em cool enough for me."

"How you know they ain't cops?" Her face crumpled into what looked like a leg cramp as she sized us up, finally narrowing her eyes she said,

"Chalk, ain't you watch TV? They could be like that Starsky and Hutch, or the Mod Squad, you never know nothin' `bout no one these days."

"The Man be shootin' live ammo, and the dude with the Elvis haircut, and pint of hooch-he be too dumb to be a cop."

"Dumb," Grinder said. "Who you callin' dumb?"

"Shut up Grinder," I said. "Look, you help us get out of here. Maybe we can do something for you."

"Damn right you do somethin' fo me," Chalk said,

"Not just some gold chains, I said." That's when I went into a speech about being from the future and all the things that were going to happen in the year 1978 and on up to 2012. How Richard Pryor and Eddie Murphy's careers progressed. I told them about Michael Jackson, James Brown, and Rap music, even breaking down the course of history and how it would yield a black U.S. President. Neither Tamina or Chalk seemed to give a shit, but when I told them that if they bet on a certain horse, Affirmed, the winning horse in today's Kentucky

Derby, they both perked up. I'd given the choice to either do well, or they could kill the three of us. And that very day I reminded them was the running of the Derby and if they wanted a score they better act quick. They looked at each other in disbelief and the woman motioned with her head to the hi fi over in the corner, it was just below a velvet painting of Jimi Hendrix. Chalk turned the station from the pulsing beat of Aretha Franklin demanding Respect to the sports channel and looked at Tamina. She had a puzzled look on her face as we all listened. Finally the broadcaster announced the time of the race.

"Race ain't runnin' till later. You sayin' you know who the winner is? You bet your life?" Tamina said.

"Yeah," I said. "You win, we win. You help us and we all get well."

"You dat crazy, huh?" Chalk said. He'd let his aviators slide down and stared at me.

"Affirmed will take first and Alydar comes in second." I said.

"I gots me someplace to hock that fine gold and place some bets. You wrong dude, you's done picked the wrong number."

"Thass right, if Chalk says your numba's up. You day edd," Tamina said, nodding her head.

"Tamina ain't givin' you no Jive," Chalk agreed. "You lie, you die." He held up a pistol and struck from what I can best recall, a cross between one very bad ass Samuel L. Jackson in that Superfly stance , and Sean Connery as James Bond.

"Not to worry Chalk," just find us a bookie. "Then, we listen to the race. After that, I'll make us all well and you'll be set for life." At that point I calculated the life expectancy of street criminals and it wasn't much greater than that of a fruit fly.

"You're on motherfucker." Chalk said.

I patted my wallet. My lucky Krugerrand was still there and maybe, just maybe, it'd bring me the sort of luck that we can only make for ourselves.

The pounding on the door was not a knock. It was the Sheriff and he wasn't looking for us, he knew where we were. It didn't occur to me at the time that no matter where Nadine, Grinder, or I were, the implanted trackers along with the mymine that was activated by the nanotechtonic rejuvenator, the N.T.R., at Beaufort's office back in nineteen fifty eight. Damn, that Sheriff had a fix on our location no matter where or when we were.

"We gotta get the fuck out of here, the law's just caught up with us."

"How you motherfucker's know it ain't some bums lookin' fo someplace to crash, huh?"

Grinder said: "Does that sound like a bum's knock?"

At that we heard the bullhorn of Sheriff Wilkens: "Come out now," and the banging continued. I could see the door begin to shatter in my mind's eye.

"Fuck it, man, we gotta split. That prick will kill us all."

"You sure 'bout that motherfucker? How I know there ain't some fat reward for turnin' you're whitey asses in?"

At that two gunshots followed by the sound of a door being kicked in echoed through the warehouse. The Sheriff must've shot the lock and would be on us in seconds.

"Follow me motherfuckers," Chalk said, raised his pistol and fired twice in the general direction of the sheriff. "Now I be's an accomplice so there best be a motherfuckin' score in here, c'mon. Follow me!"

I had my lucky Krugerrand. The time was comin' to cash it in and make my bet. All we had to do was get the fuck out of there.

We made our getaway in a tricked out Coupe deVille with a Landau top. We 'd burst through the barrier onto the street and flew past three intersections until Chalked slowed, stopped and fussed with his hair in the rear view mirror. After a few beats he turned to face the three of us sitting in the back seat and smiled, his gold rimmed front teeth glistened in the afternoon sun. There was a diamond embedded in one of them. "Now we get's down to bidness my fine white friends." He turned, and winked at Tamina in the passenger seat and put the car in drive, and we drove off slowly into the depths of the city.

Grinder nudged me in the right kidney. "Hey CP, how come I gotta ride bitch?"

"Shut the fuck up Grinder. You're lucky to be alive."

"He's right," Nadine said from across Grinder's lap.

WHY ARE WE HERE?

We had been driving for a while and the cracked window kept the smoke from Chalk's incessant Kool cigarettes from choking us. It wafted past me and out the window into the day's thermals on up into the clouds where the smoke dissipated like so many dreams vanish as a day begins. Our bets were placed and the race was long since over. We all scored and the funds disposed of as I'd seen fit. This quirk in the space-time continuum allowed me to use my knowledge of a future event to profit. Would I be struck down by some cosmic deity? Would the future change. I did not know then, nor do know today if anything can ever truly be altered or changed that has not already occurred. My proceeds were sitting nicely in an account I set up in nineteen seventy eight. I simply placed my against the odds winnings into my account and moved it into a mutual fund. The Fidelity Magellan Fund run by Peter Lynch. If I lived, I'd be living well.

I dozed off for a spell and dreamed of nothing, there was only blackness. I awoke with a sense of foreboding, not knowing why or what I was doing in this twisted chimera, which in many ways may have been part of a dream I did not have. And that is what struck me as odd, no dreams. My dreams were often vivid multicolor visions of a world where things are not just as I wish them to be, but utopic. At my home beneath the bridge I slept better than I did when I lived in a fine home, was a respected pillar of my community, and my children and my wife relied upon me as I did them. Looking back at those times, was I a better human being? I do not know. Many among my closest friends and allies have told me that I was an asshole. The fact that you do indeed meet the same people on the way down as you did on the way up was in every sense in line with my own experiences. I was down and out but quite content living as a homeless man beneath a bridge. An untouchable of sorts, free from the social bonds and responsibilities men of my age had struggled and were compelled to ascend to. It just was not for me. Some free spirit had taken over, some called it laziness, lack of motivation, cowardice, to face some manufactured notions of society. I believed that reality stayed the same, even if you didn't believe in it-had become little more than a greedy, computer driven, superficial charade. I left a fine practice and affluence, giving it up to have all of nothing. A place among the ordinary and no ties to any duty or obligation other than the bare minimum to keep me sustained. My only other working skill was that of a caddy. It's simplicity brought me to a place in nature and conscious pleasure that overrode the mental mettle ingrained as a physician which began to erode my soul. Medical dramas and mind-numbing tedium became a superfluous suffocating soliloquy. I didn't want the job, any job that chained my spirit or bent my will. So part timing it with echelons, outside the fray, made it a sport. One I could walk away from.

I looked to my left, Nadine, a woman from the future whose past was much a mystery as any I'd known. Yet there lie within her some kinetic force which drew me in but repelled me at the same time. She dozed as did my old friend and sometime colleague Neal Grinder, a doctor who'd broken more rules than most knew existed. Why was he here with me in what, by any measure would be some dream, some hallucination or other chemically induced stupor. But this jaunt through time and space and the very fact that I could fall asleep and awake, and feel and sense my very being did not suggest it to be anything other than a reality, that would go away if for a moment I stopped believing in it. The bullets were real, the longing and desire for Nadine would not, even in my wildest mental machinations evaporate. There was a genuine component at that point where all the things that happened crystallized, and this time and place were as real as life was going to get.

"Yo motherfucker," Chalk yanked his head toward me.

"You DO know where we be goin'?" It wasn't a question.

His voice had awoken Grinder and Nadine as well as drawing Tamina in the passenger seat out of her reverie. Seat-dancing, shoulder shaking, head bobbing boogie to the beat of some disco music that pulsed in some syncopated throb which was the background music for these times. Nineteen seventy eight.

"Yeah," I said.

"What dat be, motherfucker?" Chalk lit another Kool and put has hands on the steering wheel. He seemed to focus on something other than the music, he wasn't dancing in his seat.

"We're going to double back toward the city and find a guy," I said.

"You're nuts, CP. We just hit a major score, shook the Sheriff and those schvartzas are off our..."

"Shut up, Grinder," I said.

"Who you callin' show arts uh? What dat mean, some whitey talk?" Tamina said.

"Grinder's an idiot. If we don't go back to the city, we're going to get pulled over by the highway patrol, the sheriff must've called them and then we're popped."

"Maybe you right, CP. You be right about the race. But how I know this ain't a set up?" He nervously flicked his ash.

"I set you up I mizewell set myself up. I know a dude, he's a fixer. He'll make things right," I said.

"Who dat be?" Chalk said.

"His name's Beaufort, Doc Beaufort," I said. "He'll know what to do."

"You best be right motherfucker. I ain't got me no place to go with John Q on my ass and my homies knowin' I gots me all this scratch. You best be mother fucking right."

"I am right. We need to see the doctor." I said. "He's in the city."

Nadine put her hand on my thigh and I saw her nod in agreement.

Grinder leaned forward and chimed in: "Yeah, Chalk, Doc Beaufort. He's not only cool. He can do some friggin' magic."

"I needs magic I go see Mr. Johnson. Ain't no magic back in the city but the abracadabra they's gonna play on our asses we show up with all this booty," Chalk said. "But maybe you right CP, we ain't got no place to go but the country and I ain't big on the great outdoors."

Tamina got huffy: "Chalk, you goin' to listen to these white boys? A docca? What you some kinda crazy man? We got the police lookin' fo us. Chalk's crew, they gonna have the word out wantin' a piece of him, and you wants to go back to the city?" Tamina said. "You one crazy homey."

Chalk had already made up his mind and the farmland and cornfields were behind us. I could see the skyline as we drove silently toward the concrete jungle we'd narrowly escaped. The sun had begun to set and the flickering lights twinkled in the distance like a glimpse to the heavens or in our case an entirely new form of hell.

The building had not changed in its structure in twenty years but the shops had gone through several iterations and the urban decay was obvious beneath the flickering streetlights. Hookers leaned on lamp posts, winos and bums of various addictions ambled about occasionally stirring up a young thug or another. There were beat up automobiles parked aimlessly in front of fire hydrants too ragged and decayed to merit even a parking ticket. What was once the hub of a booming small town slice of Americana had become another piece of bad pie which had not only gone stale but was crawling with vile, rotting, discarded people, and wares hardly essential in nineteen seventy eight. There was a dimly lighted X-rated bookshop, video outlet, and peep show, for the local pervs on the ground floor of the two story building. The other shops which once flourished were boarded up and wore the broad strokes of street art, painted by one of the conflicting street gangs that marauded the terrain. Chalk explained the rules of the road and his pimped out ride was like a beacon of sorts. A warning that its driver was a bad motherfucker which would, for a while, keep the local hoodlumry at bay. But a clock ticked in the criminal minds and that clock began ticking the moment we parked in front of Beaufort's office.

"Well, well, well," Doc Beaufort had not aged in twenty years. He stood there beaming. Milly was at his side and she looked unchanged as well.

"Hello," Milly said. "You had best come in."

"Yes, yes. It could be a bit perilous in the hallway this time of day." Doc Beaufort led us into his office.

I looked around and somehow felt comforted in its ordinariness. In what had been a most extraordinary stretch of time from my awakening beneath the bridge, the ride with Grinder, the cornfield and crop duster, the crazed stalking sheriff, and winning the nineteen seventy eight Kentucky Derby. I was weary, and my sense of place and purpose was somewhat askew. But I had a sense of well being in this place. It hadn't changed since the cosmic registry of time read nineteen fifty eight. It had remained exactly the same as it had twenty years earlier down to the flickering x-ray view box on the wall. I reflected upon the magazines on the table in the waiting room and the dates had not changed either. For Beaufort and Milly it was very much as if time had stood still.

"Hey, snap out if young man," Beaufort broke my reverie with his cheerful, all knowing even toned voice. "I see you've met some people in your travels."

"Chalk's the name." The leather jacketed man tipped his feathered hat, smiled, displaying his grill work and held out his hand. "And this is Tamina, she's with me."

Beaufort looked at the bejeweled fingers and shook hands with the man and said: "Pleasure to meet you young man." He looked over at Tamina and gave her a slight nod and sat down behind his desk. "Please, make yourselves comfortable."

Grinder and Nadine sat across from Beaufort's large desk, Chalk and Tamina found the sofa accommodating and made themselves comfortable.

"Mmm...this is nice Doc. Ziss real leather?" Tamina asked.

"Yes it is," Beaufort said, and turned toward the open office door where Milly was standing at its threshold. I stood leaning against the wall next to her. "Why don't you get our guests some beverages."

"I could use a drink, a liquor drink, Doc," Grinder said. "Whatever it is, make mine a double."

"Well well well, seems like you've got quite a thirst young man. But I think we can arrange something for you. And your new friends, anything in particular?"

"I'd like me a Courvoisier and Coke, if you gots it?" Chalk said, taking in the sumptuous elegance of the office. "You a classy guy, I figure you gots to have the good stuff, umm hmm. One for my lady, too."

"Of course." Beaufort nodded at Milly.

Milly arched an eyebrow, looked over at Chalk and Tamina, smiled briefly then glanced at me, shooting me a quick wink.

Ten minutes later two empty snifters set on the side table beside the sofa where Chalk and Tamina slept.

"Had to make sure nobody from nineteen seventy eight returns to this place boys. Things like that can disrupt the space-time continuum and wreak havoc for a future that's already occurred. I wouldn't want for Milly and I to vaporize into the realm of nonexistence on a turn of the phrase rendered in here being accidentally leaked into the public realm now would we?"

"Jeez, that can really happen?" Grinder said, patting himself down making sure he was still all put together.

"You betcha," Beaufort said. "Now tell me, what you've been up to? The Sheriff followed you from fifty eight a few hours ago. It's a good thing too, folks were gettin' shook up, seein' the military 'round these parts ain't particularly good for the likes of us time transplanters, right Milly?"

Milly nodded in agreement.

Nadine reported the events of the day and watched Beaufort's response.

He sat there, behind the desk and seemed to ponder the possibilities. Finally he leaned forward, his elbows on the desk, his fingers forming a cage. He spoke slowly in an even tone: "We're going to have to get you out of this time, and soon. You should know that old Dr. Duss, the chiropodist, took whatever you told him about the future and has become a nationally known surgeon and expert of sorts. He's a multi-millionaire today, thanks to you boys. Now that's just fine, but he moved out of the building here maybe ten or so years ago and we sort of took over the space. You see, he was meant to be here, at this time in history. When he moved off, it created a temporal vacuum which needed to be filled. Wasn't much but it had to be wrapped up lickety split. Good thing we just nabbed the space when we did. The T.B.I. sent along a warning about that. You boys can't go changing history. These folks Chalk and his girlfriend. I doubt if they'll be missed, so we can just have them awake in their vehicle without any memory of being here. Milly slipped them one of our forgetaboutit concoctions. That's no problem. But the Sheriff won't see it that way, neither will the T.B.I. And with that Kentucky Derby thing, you may very well have set off a cascade of events which have not yet been realized in the year you came back from. Hmm...no matter what it is, Sheriff Wilkens is going to want to blame Milly, Nadine, and me. He's going to insist the T.B.I. send us back to the future.

HIS future. Not good, not good at all. We like it here."

"I'm staying with CP," Nadine said.

"Well, well, well, Nadine this presents a most curious paradox." Beaufort put the palms of his hands together forming a steeple. "Are you certain of this, Nadine?"

"Yes," she said. "Are you OK with this CP?"

I looked at her shrugged my shoulders and smiled. Damn I actually smiled-Hell yes, I wanted this.

They, Nadine, Grinder, Beaufort and Milly had read my thoughts. So this was going to be the way it was.

"You do know it is only a matter of time, perhaps a few moments until the Sheriff finds his way here? We'd best load these two into their car and give them a little wake up shove and set them on their way. Don't worry, they'll be just fine. This community can be a very comfortable place for the Derby winner to start a new career. They'll both awake tomorrow with scads of cash money and a bit of a headache for which the woman will insist upon seeing a doctor for. I'll set them up just swell and in a few weeks time they'll be regular pillars of the community. It's truly amazing what can be done through pharmaceutical intervention."

Beaufort and Milly stood at the door to the stairway leading up to the office and watched us lug the Derby winners down the stairs to the car. They stood like sentinels, as if knowing something was astir yet unable, or perhaps upon reflection unwilling to tamper with what time may reveal. I pondered this as I set Chalk in the driver's seat and set his limp palms on the faux leather coated steering wheel, flicking the car deoderizer in the shape of a pine tree with my finger. I looked over at Grinder and Nadine, who'd just finished placing Tamina in the passenger seat hesitate, look at each other, and both agreeing that positioning her unconscious body more naturally nuzzled up against the pimp might be more appropriate. Yeah, I thought, maybe the marauding street thugs, muggers, winos, and whores, would think they were an item. Perilous item at that, ha. Maybe Chalk would wake up and find Tamina to be his one and only. They'd get married and move off to some promised land suburb, have lots of babies and Chalk would build an empire with his Derby dollars. I didn't consider that the future may have already been written or that any change to a past may have some impact no matter how tiny or how grand. I reflected upon Chaos theory, how the beat of a butterflies wings thousands and thousands of miles away could strike up a Tsunami on the other side of the globe. Eh, I thought, looking over at a satisfied pair of time travelers wrapping up their chore not fully cognizant that it was Doc Beaufort who suggested we take these folks and do what we did with them. There must have been a reason, a cause, a purpose. Nadine was grinning in that ready to say what do you think sort of way. Grinder was nervously looking from side to side as if all hell would break loose if he didn't check things out as frequently as he did.

Grinder hadn't taken his second step when the screeching sound of an automobile's tires turning a corner cried out like an angry bird of prey swooping from its perch. I looked up to see a police car, behind the wheel I could make out the Stetson. Hell was about to break loose.

"My, my, my, not such perfect timing. He's early." Beaufort held up a small object and pressed something, a switch, a button, who knew but Beauf and Milly?

There was a high pitched sound. Within a nanosecond the atmosphere changed, as if gravity lapsed and the space we occupied no longer existed in any way it had ever done before. The world was in slow time, like watching a disaster or an accident where everything happens in a compressed manner. Like it would never end until something awful, hideous, or tragic, ended that moment. But that didn't happen, no. A crisp evening breeze whipped up and a shimmering wall, a door of sorts, appeared on the sidewalk. I looked toward the squad car and the Sheriff was already sprinting toward us, gun drawn.

"Hold it right there, all of you!" Royal Wilkens shouted and I heard the gun cock.

"Run, CP, run!" Grinder shouted.

"Follow Beaufort," Nadine's thoughts echoed in my mind. And then I saw Doc Beaufort, he stood there like a pillar from another time, another space with some gadget in his hands. He was smiling.

"Like I always say, if you can't make it to the cornfield, bring the field to you," Beaufort said. "C'mon you ninnies we've got but a smidge to get out of here." The Doc was standing at the edge of the portal. Milly had already crossed the threshold and through my mind's eye saw her evaporate into who knew where.

Nadine and Grinder followed, throwing themselves into an abyss just as the first shot rang out. I could see a bullet penetrate this very surreal space we were in.

Beaufort looked at me, we locked eyes and he said: "We only have a moment."

He held his hand out like a maitre d' at a fine restaurant but the only thing I saw being served up was another bullet. It hung there in that place where time stands still, and I stared at it mesmerized like a deer in the headlights. Beaufort's words broke my trance: "Just move young fella this lapse won't last much longer," and he shoved me into the portal. He was right behind me. I turned to look at him, and the portal shut with a pneumatic thump. There was no Beaufort, only darkness and the world as it had been. All time and space spun madly, and I wondered what was happening. I do not recall what was going through my mind, but at the time I swear it may have been a bullet?

As the world began to shut down, I felt a pain, an icy hot pain like none I've felt before, I saw the outlines of my friends fade and knew that we occupied another space, another time. The Sheriff, I only imagined, was on the other side. The world, my world, changed again. It was as if a switch was clicked. A million stars exploded and the earth heaved a tremendous thrust, opened up and swallowed us whole. And like that, it was over. I felt like I'd woken from a hectic dream, but; it was no dream at all. Just a very long journey in a fraction of a second. I can't say I was dazed, but I looked at my friends and saw nothing. Not one thing at all.

1928

There was another thump and I felt the air sucked out of me like an elephant dropped a few stories onto my chest. Magenta, ice, heat, blurry pain, and the outlines of reality, whatever that was started to fall into place. Finally I heard the voices. Familiar voices.

Nadine and Grinder were speaking aloud and I was on my feet and the sun was shining. My right palm was pressed against a door. We were on a street in a town that I had never seen, or had I seen it at a different time in history? The cars were right out of an old gangster movie and chuck-a-lucked down the busy road, beep beep beeping away. The road was narrow but the street was a crowded street. There were no traffic lights and the buildings were right out of an Architectural Digest of a daguerreotype age. Nadine was wearing a short skirt that had a Roaring Twenties look to it, her hair, short in the back, long at the sides, her decolletage was adorned with a string of pearls. She had a headband on and blood red lipstick. My head may have throbbed and I couldn't piece together where we were but could feel another part of my anatomy aching as well.

"CP," Nadine said. "Are you all right?" She held a cigarette holder with an unlit smoke in one dark gloved hand that went all the way up her arm to her elbow. She wrapped her fingers around my shoulder and clutched it hard with the other.

"Asshole." Grinder said. "We had to lug you from the cornfield, find some threads and get our shit together dragging your sorry ass was like dead meat because you were fucking out of it. Shit CP, you been hittin' the Sterno a bit hard, especially back there in '78. Winnin' the Derby like that and givin' Wilkens the slip..."

"What happened?" I said. "Jeez those threads, Grinder. Look at you. You look like you spent a wad at the Ralph Lauren Gangsters are us shop. What did you do, raid the wardrobe section for clothes from the last Untouchables Movie?"

"I wish," Grinder said. "This fine suit is courtesy of Nadine. She had some era dollars with her and the three of us looked so out of synch with the 20's-the farmer who drove us into town thought we were foreigners. We stopped off and got these spiffy duds."

Grinder did a full Veronica showing off his stylish suit finishing it with a two hand intro of Nadine, who looked stunning. As for me? They must have dressed me in late Elliot Ness because I caught a glimpse of myself in the window of a little soda fountain/general store and saw a guy in a dark suit, Fedora and shoes with spats. "You had to add the spats, Grinder. Jeez, plain shoes would have been just fine."

"Let's have something to drink," Nadine said, shoving me into the sepia toned shop.

The shop was part grocery store, pharmacy, soda fountain, and there was a man behind the counter. He must have been the soda jerk. He had on a crisp looking white shirt rolled up just so and a visored cap on as if he were a card dealer at some casino. He wore an apron and a smile about as genuine as a soy burger. His teeth were long, straight and jagged. Dentistry must not have been much the rage. Noticing the levers of something on tap I considered a beer, but realizing it was the era of prohibition I said: "How about a coke?"

The bartender-clerk or whatever the guy was, tightened his apron string, scurried over to a place behind the puke green counter, and drew up a tall glass of fluid and placed it in front of me.

"Coca Cola!" He smiled broadly. "Pure drink of natural flavors," he said, folding his arms across his chest. "You folks visiting?"

I looked from side to side. There was a wooden phone booth to my left and shelves of merchandise behind me and to my right was more counter, and a rack of nick nacks. There was no one else was in the shop except Grinder who was checking out the goods, and Nadine who just entered the phone booth. She picked up the part of the phone you listen with, and dialed once, twice, maybe three times, and looked over at me and shook her head. Finally she was chatting to someone.

"Pure drink of natural flavors?" I said, taking a sip. It tasted like warm sugar water.

"Yep yep, it is old sport. Finest beverage in the land if you know what I mean. That there is this years slogan from Coca Cola."

"Whoopie doo, buddy. This tastes pretty crummy."

The jerk frowned as if someone rained on a parade that wasn't being held today.

Grinder joined me at the counter and asked for a pack of Chesterfields. "And I'll take some matches too."

Out of nowhere, at least to the soda jerk fetching the smokes, Nadine appeared. She'd wrapped up her call and took a seat next to me, gave me a nudge and said: "I just spoke with a friend." Looking back, I think it was more for the benefit of browntooth the soda jockey than it was for me. She faced the clerk and held out her cigarette to be lit.

"The Doc said to deal us in," she said it in a cool fuck you asshole tone.

The jerk lost a shade or two of pale, fake smiled and said: "The Doc?"

"Doc Beaufort," she said.

Nadine placed a card on the counter, it was the Queen of Hearts.

The soda jerk dropped another shade of pale, held up the card and looked over at Nadine, then at Grinder and rested his watery eyes on me. He looked edgy. "I guess that you folks are all right," the man said. "Come on, the game's in the back."

"What game?" Grinder said.

"Shut up, moron. You might have on a nice suit but you still sound like an idiot," I said.

"Hey, dickhead, I saved your life back there. That bullet may have missed you but something threw you for a loop." Grinder said.

"It was the portal," Nadine burst in. "He turned to look back. You aren't supposed to look back."

"You're not supposed to look back?" I said.

"The past, CP. The past has passed. Even if it hasn't happened yet. You can't look into it," she said.

Damn did she look good. I wanted her then. I knew I'd always want her. I just nodded and grinned. She stared into my eyes. I returned the gaze. "Come on CP, we've got a card game to attend. I think you'll enjoy the company."

I followed her then, and I knew that I'd follow her anywhere.

"Looks like sombody's got a crush," Grinder was shoving me from behind.

"Fuck you Grinder," I said.

The soda jerk pressed some switch and a panel slid open behind the counter. I could hear the sound of music, maybe jazz or something like it, and chatter, laughter and people up to some sort of partying. "I hope you enjoy yourselves," he said.

We let him escort us into the secret chamber party room. On the way, I stopped and asked him what his name was.

"They call me The Proprietor," he said. "I'm with The Organization."

The secret room was more a grand ballroom, gambling casino, mega bar, than some little hideout where roaring twenty somethings sat about drinking cheap booze. It was an elaborately appointed Gatsbyesque casino with roulette tables, slot machines and black jack tables. At one end of the room was a long Mahogany bar and a row of bottles as distinct and foreign as at any bar in 2012. In fact it could have been the twenty first century but for one major difference, a cloud of thick smoke hung in the air over the gambling tables and everyone was smoking. There was a stage and a band and the music was that of Duke Ellington right out of the Cotton Club. I was stunned by the sound and how it carried and blended with the sounds of the crowd. Laughter, chatter of all things new and modern. As if they, the people, frequenting this place might have been the same sort of folks you'd see muzzing about an Apple store all smarmy and hip. Yuppies at society's precipice, doing all the in things yet in an era where they'd hardly blink at the notion of things to come. Everyone was as far from my comfort zone regarding striking up a conversation as Antarctica, yet as close as a foot or so away. One person seemed to have a spotlight on him, maybe it was something which shone only in my mind's eye. He stood out like a man who'd been there, done it, and seen it all. He was sitting on a bar stool stirring his drink with a most unusual swizzle stick. I'd recall later the uniqueness of it because it would be pointed out to me. But the man was Doc Beaufort and the woman at his side decked out in the fashion of the day, like Nadine, and looking just as stunning was Milly. She stared at us and smiled.

"C'mon over here. We've been waiting for you." Milly said.

The Proprietor escorted us to the bar, held up a shaky hand to the bartender, an ancient African American with silver hair and a spray of freckles across his face that reminded me of Morgan Freeman. I thought of him as Red from the Shawshank Redemption movie. The way he stood there with the presence of a man who had seen it all. But for one reason or another decided to just stay out of it, taking pleasure and pride of purpose in the way he scoured the glass in his hand with a dirty bar rag and looked over at the Proprietor. His gaze was in some way menacing, knowing, and a hint of: If you screw with me, I will fuck you up. I liked him immediately and gave him the props, nodding in the way you'd nod at someone who's been there, done that and seen it all. Something told me he was that man.

I just stood there and watched as the Proprietor said to the black man: "Get them whatever they like, Negro Jim."

If a few words were ever spoken depicting a snarky, pretentious weasel, and I may have heard them at one point or another in my life, I heard them more clearly and decisively at that point, as if they'd never been spoken before. And they were in a degrading tone as ever was.

"Yes massuh," the black man said. He fake-smiled and placed the bar rag on the counter firmly as if it may have been a last straw, yet it wasn't, at least not yet. Negro Jim turned to face the Proprietor and spoke in an even tone of a knowingly disgusted man.

"Sure," he said. It sounded as if it came from high above and if it didn't make all of time stand still for anyone else in this grand cotillion of a gaming parlor, it did for me. If one word spoken could describe a generation I may have just heard it.

"They're with the Doc," Proprietor said. His upper lip had beads of perspiration and his eyes shifted from side to side before settling on the black man. "Get to it."

The black man tossed the bar rag over his shoulder and locked eyes with The Proprietor and smirked knowingly. The Proprietor seemed in some way frightened not so much by what could happen today, but what may happen in the future. He feared the black man, that was obvious to me, not just for what he knew, but for the look on his face. The bartender had a glimpse of what things could be, but dare I mention that some day a black man would be the President of the United States?

"No," Nadine read my mind. "It's nineteen twenty eight and the President is Calvin Coolidge. Don't forget it." She smiled. I wanted to take her to a closet and screw her silly.

She must have read those thoughts too, because as dark as it was, she blushed pointing her chin at the Doc.

Beaufort must have gotten a directors version of history's final cut as he was dressed as elegantly as James Bond may have been in any of the features not even imagined by any of Ian Flemming's iterations.

"Well, well, well, boys," he held up his hand and looked at a wrist watch, grinned and turned to face us. "Just in time. It's nice to see you all here at Cap's Place."

"Cap's Place?" I said.

"Yes," Milly said. "It's a speakeasy. I think you'll find some of the other people here quite compelling." She took a drag from her holdered cigarette, leaving a layer of blood red lipstick on it and draped a long luxurious arm across Beaufort's elegant suit coat.

"Who the fuck are these people?" Grinder was looking around the room.

"Jeez, Grinder, can you ever shut the hell up?" I said.

"Is that fucking Al Capone?" Grinder said.

"You best not stare Grinder," Doc Beaufort said."Al does not like to be stared at."

"And that motherfucker, is that Thomas fucking Edison?" Grinder's jaw nearly shattered his knee caps.

"Grinder, Grinder, Grinder. Did you ever think that there are reasons outside of your streams of consciousness which exist that don't concern you?" Beaufort said, taking a sip from his drink. "Yes that is Thomas, and the man in the corner sipping a beverage is an old rival of his, Nikola Tesla. They had a real spat over a few AC/DC things some time ago. Old Nikola is about to have some of his theories solidified for his electric ignition switch for gas engines which Henry Ford, another fellow who should be arriving soon will find most delightful.

"What's he talkin' about, CP?" Grinder's drink arrived and he chugged it, held his glass up for another and looked at me.

We both stared at Albert Einstein who was rubbing a hand on the buttocks of one of the scantily clad flappers. He had won a Nobel prize back in 1921 for his work on the photoelectric effect. I knew he was working on his unified field theory and that Tesla hated his guts. No wonder they seemed to exchange some brittle vibes between them. Einstein wasn't supposed to be in the United States in 1928. That was the year he had some sort of nervous breakdown, the history books called it a physical collapse as did Wikipedia. But who could believe what you could read on the internet in 2012? I watched him as he looked over at us, raked his fingers through that lock of hair and came over to us.

"Well well well, Al, how are you doing today?" Doc Beaufort said.

"Me? I'm fine. I don't know vat is vit dis crezzy country here but zizz probition ting it makes the nutsy Germans laugh like a big comedy."

"It is quite silly, Albert, yes indeed it is. How is that new theory you're working on?" Beaufort said as he reached into his pocket and removed a slip of paper. "This may help you with your work, Al."

I was sitting next to Doc Beaufort staring at a fortyish Albert Einstien, Grinder was oblivious as usual and Nadine edged closer, drawn in to the conversation.

"This is Nadine," Milly said. "She's with CP, another doctor friend of Beaufort. "What would you say if I told you he was a time traveler? He came here with his buddy to change the future." She pointed her chin at the rotgut swilling Grinder.

"I vood say dat Zee Pee is full of ze sheisser undt zo are you, but ze voman iz very much in ze presentum, no?"

With that, Albert Einstein put his hand on Nadine's butt. She jerked and I could see her blush. Einstein squeezed her ass and the look on Nadine's face was a mix of humiliation, horror and the sort of titillation that accompanies meeting a movie star. I smacked Einstein's hand away. "She's with me Al," I said.

Einstein stepped back, held up his hands and shook his head. "Not a big deal Zee Pee. ziss vas an example of my relativity zeory. Vun second on a beautiful voman's ezz is like an hour vit vun's hand in a flame."

"What's that guy talkin' about?" Grinder said.

"It's all relative, boys. A second of pleasantness in one place can seem like an eternity in another. It all is dependent upon ones frame of reference," Beaufort said.

"Very tru, very, very tru," Einstein said. "I vill have to remember zat."

"You ready for the card game Al?" Beaufort added.

"You betcha."

"Won't be long now. I'd try and avoid Nikola over there. He's still steaming about the whole Nobel prize thing," Beaufort said.

"Steam shmeam I plan on cleaning him out at ze poker table." Einstein said and then turned to me. "Don't vorry about ze girl, she's vit you and I vuss juss messin' mit you."

We shook hands and I watched him walk away toward another flapper I supposed. He was studying the slip of paper Beaufort gave him. He had that look of someone who just had an aha moment. He held up a finger as if to punctuate that moment.

I turned back toward the counter, bowed my head and recall considering the people in the room.

"I think we're here for a reason." I said. I was looking at my drink on the counter, the ice cubes floated to the top and the swizzle stick was the same sort Beaufort had. There was an orange stone of sorts encrusted in it. Beaufort must have read my thoughts because he turned to me and stared.

"That's not an ordinary stone CP. And you thought the name Flemming, didn't you?"

"I did. I was thinking about the author."

"I just visited with another Fleming, Alexander. Yes the fellow who developed penicillin. I borrowed a bit and my old friend Thomas had a bit of the strep throat. Yes, yes he did. And I gave him a bit. It's not his time to pass yet. The streptococcal infection would surely have done him in. He'll be fine now."

"You gave him penicillin?" I said. "That's changing history, isn't it?"

"Of course he did," Milly said. "Why else would we be here? Did you ever try to find a good internet connection in 1928?"

"Sometimes we need to modify the past for a better future," Beaufort said. "Yes, yes, yes, indeed."

Milly took a drag from her cigarette, shrugged and smiled.

"You boys know Tommy B. don't you?" Beaufort said.

"That friggin' osteopathetic asshole? What the fuck is he doing here?" Grinder said admiring himself in the mirror behind the bar. He looked at himself proudly hitching his thumbs in the lapels of the high couture of the day.

"Yes," Beaufort said. "Tommy has been taking all sorts of liberties. He settled back in your time, but things, as things most often do, do not go according to plan. So he's here."

"What the fuck's that asshole doing here?" Grinder said. Leaning in to get a better look at himself and then stepping back watching himself gavotte.

I thought that if some men dressed in some hokey celebration of self that's supposed to free him from his caste, it didn't for my friend. Grinder, despite the elegance of his stylish attire proved the adage: You can dress them up but you can't take them anywhere. There was no set of clothes that could conceal or even change the essence of the man, rather revealing it, as though a spotlight shone on him, the essential smart ass I've known as Neal Grinder. I looked away from my idiot friend and stared at Beaufort. "A card game? Let me guess, Tommy's dealing."

"Yes indeed," Beaufort said. "Tommy has a card game to play and the stakes are quite high."

"Yeah? Well we can read minds and already know he's a crumb. Friggin' Capone'd be a sore loser, eh? Might just bust a cap in old Tommy B," Grinder said.

"Al Capone, or for that matter no one can do anything to change what will be. However if WE do not intervene, the current of history will not be quite so generous and perhaps all time will have been altered."

"Cease to exist?" Grinder lost a few shades of bluster.

"Yes," Milly said.

"We'll be using the Tarot deck for some poker." Beaufort went on. He spoke as seriously as if someone might not just die but that the weight of the world would soon be upon us.

"I guess the stakes are up there," I said.

"Let's put it this way, CP. If things don't go precisely as they are supposed to, we'll all cease to exist."

With that, Doc Beaufort held up a hand, pinched his fingers together, held them up to his lips and blew. "Poof. All of everything will be gone."

EX PARTE CONVERSATION IN A BATHROOM WITH DOC BEAUFORT IN 1928

"I suppose there's a reason why we're going to use Tarrot cards to play poker?" I said, finishing my drink.

"Yes," Beaufort plucked the swizzle stick out of his glass and put it in his jacket pocket, raised his head and said. "We need to talk."

"Explain the way things are, Beauf. It's time," Milly said. "Grinder have another drink, Nadine and I will keep you company while they talk."

"What's going on?" I said.

"Well, well, well, CP. I am going to borrow you from your friends and you and I will have a private conversation before we begin any games of chance. I do not particularly enjoy leaving many things at all to such things as chance." With that, Doc Beaufort firmly gripped my arm above the elbow and led me to the men's room. There was an attendant in there who he handed some money to, and shooed away. Beaufort checked the stalls, empty. Went over to the lavatory entry, locked the door and leaned against the sink counter and grinned as though he were about to reveal the meaning of life, the location of the Lost Arc, or some National Treasure. He must have read my mind because he said aloud. "Close, young man, very close."

And this is when Doc Beaufort told me how and why we were here, and what may happen if I did not do as I was meant to do. To carry that mythical package across the street, to be that one small cog in the mechanism of the universe, to make it work just fine and the gears of reality as we know it remain oiled. The following is what he described...

"I had an interesting conversation with Thomas Edison a couple days ago."

Beaufort told me that he popped in from the future to visit Thomas Edison and that's why he, Edison was here today. Edison travelled from Fort Myers, his Florida home and laboratory to partake in this game of chance. There was something integral to history that needed to be done. Beaufort knew that it would be a tough sell, explaining to Thomas Edison what he needed to explain, but did so nevertheless equipped with what Edison respected more than life itself, science. Edison was known for his adage: "All that is, can be explained along material lines." In essence the basis for all of Edison's work and creations were grounded in science.

A few days before Beaufort's arrival, he sent a confederate of sorts to visit Edison, to peak his interest. It was a person from the year 2070 who promised he could read Edison's mind. The visitor sent by Beaufort knew of Edison's fascination with the paranormal and the mysterious stranger-Beaufort's man had Edsion write some notes on a slip of paper. Then without ever looking at the paper, the stranger from 2070 rattled off what Edison had written. Edison thought he'd trip the stranger up, but the stranger repeated it again and again. Finally Edison asked the stranger if there was anything better for a storage battery than nickel-hydroxide and the stranger, knowing what was available at that time said: "No Mr. Edison there is nothing better." Then he left Edsion's laboratory never to be seen by Edison again. The stranger left one message, he whispered in Thomas Edison's ear. The stranger told him that another stranger would arrive in the garden within the week at his experimental laboratory in

Fort Myers, Florida. That he, a Doctor, would provide him with grand ideas, and provide a cure of sorts for whatever ailed him, and reveal secrets which would allow him to develop a project that was of utmost secrecy. No one had known, not even his private diary reflected the spirit communication device. Edision was shocked by the stranger's words, he immediately put into play the document. Unbeknownst to historians, the stranger infected Thomas Edison with the Gram positive streptococcal bacteria that would develop into strep throat within the week

Edison put in orders for the battery, he did so according to the Doc Beaufort's advices and assistance.

As Beaufort explained it to me in the bathroom at Cap's place in the year 1928, after having someone visit Edison, Beaufort showed up.

Two days later Doc Beaufort appeared in Fort Myers, in Thomas Edison's botanical gardens. Edison was not surprised, Beaufort explained. "The fellow was expecting me. And he was sick as hell. I had just popped in on Alexander Fleming, said hello and filled a syringe with penicillin. I knew that Edison would need it."

Which, he apparently, according to Doc Beaufort, did. How easy would it have been for Beaufort to just pop in on Alexander Fleming? Would I bother to ask a man who gave me the ability to travel through time, to read minds? No. Some things you just take at face value, and this was one of them.

So Doc Beaufort explained to me then how he began to endear himself to the inventor, administering the new medicine for an illness, which surely Beaufort told me, would have killed him. Did Doc Beaufort have some knowledge of alternative realities where all things imagined could have actually occurred? I though this to myself.

By helping Edison with his botanical gardens at the Ft. Myers lab he started with a simple bit of advice regarding rubber and then explained to him how his light bulb would change the world. But Edison had more pressing problems that day. Harvey Firestone, whose rubber was used on Model T's and A's was in short supply, and Edison had been working feverishly to develop a new strain of rubber. Beaufort gave him one of many formulas that day, Edison's rubber problem was solved. It was then that Beaufort told me that he instilled in Edison a way to finance grand things for a future he may, by way of his spirit capture device, be able to see. Edison, the skeptic he was, played along. Knowing that any idea was just that, until proven wrong. He was not going to pass up on a man who could not only read his mind but solve his problems as well.

And this is why we were here in 1928 about to play a game of chance with historical figures using some mystical magical material as chips. Those embedded swizzle sticks contained the very precursors to the cyclic nucleotide, nanotechnologic innovation and all things that made eternal life, time travel and everything we were, possible. And Tommy B. was willing to gamble it in the hopes, according to Beaufort, of taking over Al Capone's network in the years ahead to be behind the rise of the Third Reich, Pearl Harbor, the Korean Conflict, the death of the Kennedy brothers and all of everything that had an impact on history, at least as I knew it.

THOMAS EDISON AND ETERNAL LIFE

At some point Edison told Beaufort that he had come to the conclusion that there is no supernatural, that all there is...can be explained along material lines.

The very presence of Doc Beaufort in Edison's life provoked Edison to later be quoted by Forbes Magazine about the incident with a stranger: "What man did this strange thing (he did not mention the injection). That is the reason why I say we may develop a new sense, or more than one new sense in the course of our life time, but it will be material."

Later in his life, Edison would deny this. But at the time of his death he had been working on a project that Doc Beaufort suggested. His diary reflects what that project was. For your information and some insight into the mysterious ways of Doc Beaufort and perhaps why me and Grinder got caught up in these things, I'll read from Thomas Edison's diary, something that was given to me by Milly. It read as follows:

"If our personality survives then it is strictly logical and scientific to assume that it retains memories, intellect, and other faculties and knowledge, that we acquire on earth. I am inclined to believe that our personalities in the hereafter will be able to affect matter. If this reasoning be correct, then we can evolve an instrument so delicate as to be effected, moved, or manipulated by our personality as it survives in the next life, such by scientific means."

Later Edison concluded that if we ever succeeded in establishing communication beyond our life times it will be by scientific means.

In 1933 an article in Modern Mechanics Magazine described a secret meeting Edison had, in the late 1920s. A gathering of Edison, Firestone, Henry Ford, William Flagler, and a young Albert Einstein. At this meeting of sorts, Edison demonstated a photo-electric cell that revealed, what some might describe as a bit off, in many ways a so-called, spirit in a beam of light. The writings of this event are sketchy at best but the documents amassed by Doc Beaufort for my review that day in 1928, at Cap's place pretty much summed up the fact that Edison had been working on his spirit communication device but that the acutal apparatus had not been at all described in any public literature or ever patented. In fact the material was largely nonexistent anywere, with, the exception of resources Beaufort had at his disposal. Edison did write publicly at some point that: "I have been at work for some time building an apparatus to see if it is possible for personalities which have left this earth to communicate with us." Of course he denied this as anything but a joke.

However Edison 's spirit communication device, may have been merely speculative to Edison early on, but his propitious meeting with Doc Beaufort provided the essential ingredient to make it work. The machine, the spirit communication device was originally in Edison's thoughts to be something akin to a storage battery. Something that could capture what he believed was that the human body had an energy, and that energy "may scatter after death." Edison believed that a human had one hundred trillion life units that scatter and that somehow he could capture them.

Doc Beaufort stepped away from the lavatory counter, reached into the side pocket of his sports coat and pulled out the swizzle stick. He fiddled around with it for a few seconds, finally popping out the amber crystal and held it up to my eye level before putting it in my hand. It felt odd, almost electric and seemed to emit some energy of its own. Maybe that's when I knew it was more than just a pretty stone. He took it back, reinserted it and held it up as if it was a talisman.

HYGRONTINUM THE ESSENTIALS

"This is part molybdenum, part hygrontinum and a whole lot of bull shit. Hygrontinum aka Hygro, has not, nor ever will be on the periodic chart of the elements. It was used in the 2050s as a conduit in the manufacture of the mymine nucleotide which was integrated into my DNA to prevent me from being afflicted with cancer and prevent me from aging. We discussed this in 1958. As the years passed the HYGRO, named after a false bursa that covers pressure points because it IS a false buffer of sorts is integrated into the makings of this special material needed to be directed via the supercomputers that right now are overhead."

"In nineteen twenty eight?" I said, staring at the orangish crystal.

"They have been updated and modified in the years beyond 5772. Even our 2070 technology is based on something that didn't exist until explorers travelled to the future's future."

He must have seen the puzzled look on my face.

"No need to concern yourself with that now. Our concerns are today, right here, right now."

"I'm all ears, Doc." I said.

Edison was working on an eternal life storage battery. He succeeded in developing one in 1929. There is no record of it and it captured the thoughts, ideas, impulses, and emotions, of human beings for all time to be stored in special containers, which Edison maintained. In fact, we still have his. He did not know how to capture the spirit beam, he liked to call it that, as it came from a dying human. We learned how to do that procedure in the 2060s but that's not here nor there. The Hygrontinum is what counts today. The Hygro is what Tommy B is gambling with."

"What about the T.B.I.?"

"Right now the Time Bureau of Investigation is at risk, and the development of The Organization can be altered in it's nascent stages if the card game does not go as we need it to."

"Wait a second, who's the <u>we</u>?" I said. I got to admit I was puzzled and maybe a bit sore, thinking that Beaufort was trying to use me to fuck over history. Then again there was the girl, but there was always the girl.

"The T.B.I. is a fascist group that controls all society. If they really do take charge we're all fucked, tracked and live under their umbrage. On the other hand if <u>The Organization</u>.wins, there'll be at least a chance for relocating at different times in history. Trust me on this, the future's no holiday. What's left of the earth isn't worth living on, and the computers are beyond what anyone can imagine."

"Try me."

Beaufort was noticabaly tetched. "Listen CP remember when the iPhone's and all that crap came out? They were the cats meow and everyone had to have them. Banks had every detail of your life, and your medical records stored, shared, and scattered. Amplify your loss of privacy by a billion and think of the future. The T.B.I. cannot win this poker game.

If they do history will be controlled by a computer network that will enslave all of us."

"Computers as our masters." I said milling over what he said.

"Listen to me now CP, and listen to me as if all you know or ever will know, or love depends on it.

Computer generated commands, duels, arguments, and battles, will always rely on computers. There will be a perpetual stalemate and no one human will ever win. At best we can escape the computers to simpler times B.C., before computers."

He held up the swizzle stick. If Tommy B wins tonight the T.B.I. will rule the world for centuries. If Al Capone wins he'll own the T.B.I. and the permutation of future will be people like a hybridization of Royal Wilkens and Cyberdine from the Terminator movies on steroids. If Edison and I take the pot The Organization will be formed and funded and some modicum of humanity will suffice it to say, be as human as it can be."

"What's that supposed to mean?"

"Everything costs money CP. Those computers up in space weren't cheap. I will favor Edison with a device that he along with his friends Henry Ford and Harvey Firestone will utilize in every automobile ever made. A certain signal will be installed in all vehicles in the 1980s onward reminding people to take their vehicles to be inspected. The Check Engine Light will be linked to the HYGRO that Edison will use to develop a luminous indicator that can only be shut off by a device of mine, by one of OUR mechanics. Mechanics who will pay a tribute to The Organization-OUR organization. This is your destiny. The bank accounts are established around the world and the deposits from mechanics will go directly to them. All you have to do is win this game and leave the bartering and establishment of the CEL society to me and Edison. It's all been prearranged.

"Talk about high stakes poker." I said.

"No matter what, Capone cannot win, neither can Tommy B." Beaufort held up the crystal embedded swizzle stick again.

"If I read you right, that means I may have to cheat a bit." I said.

"If you want to live, you have to follow my lead," Beaufort said, returning the swizzler to his pocket.

THE GAME IS ON AND WE'RE PLAYING FOR HYGRONTINUM

I must be dreaming...I said to myself as Beaufort banged on the bathroom door shouting that we were stuck in there.

He glanced over his shoulder and said to me: "CP, when we get to the card table, take a seat, don't stare and don't show any emotion as if you give a darn one way or another. You'll know what to do when you do it."

"I don't know what you're talking about? You're talking in riddles." I said, just as the lavatory door knob turned and the ancient attendant looked at us like a pair of queers or something.

"You boys doin' aw raht?" The attendant said holding out an arm with a shoe buffing cloth draped over the forearm.

"We're fine, young man." Beaufort placed a twenty dollar bill in his hand. "Now go back to work."

"Sure, whatever you say, sir," he looked at the bill, pursed his lips and gave slight nod. "Thank you boss man.

Gangsters, the ballroom was now filled with them. They must have been Al Capone's posse. The gangster also had a bevy of fine looking young women fawning all over him as he sat at the card table, stogie in hand.

"Yeah," Capone said to everyone and no one. "Let's get this game going. I'm a busy man, see." The gangster smiled at his bodyguards, ladies, and all around him in that see what a great guy I am, sort of way.

There were two tough guy fellows on either side of him all suited up in the Armani for Wise Guys garb of the day. I could tell by the bulges in their clothes they were packing heat and it wasn't for the flappers. No, the Tommy gun one of them held was a warning not to mess with Big Al.

"I play a fair game of cards boys. Don't let the heat throw you offf, see." Big Al said.

Doc Beaufort nodded silently.

Shit, I said to myself. What the hell was I in for now?

Einstein, Edison, Flagler, Beaufort, Grinder, and me were seated at the green felt covered poker table. A lamp hung overhead and the dealer Tommy B. stood there like some sentinel. He wore a white shirt with rubber bands holding up his sleeves and one of those visor caps that old-time card dealers wore. He had a huge deck of cards that frankly gave me the creeps. Tarot cards? I don't know about anyone else, but something about a deck of cards that can read the future and freak people out bothered me. Grinder nudged my side and shook his head in that, I don't know about this shit way that people do, but seventy eight cards is a lot of cards to be playing poker with. We were still waiting on someone. We'd already gotten word that Henry Ford was not going to play and that the last player hadn't sat down yet. That someone was Nikola Tesla. He approached the table and was looking around more pissed off than pleased to be here and Al Capone looked over at him. The two men locked eyes.

"Hey sit down goombah, see, we got a card game to play. Come on sit down right here next to me Nikola."

At that moment the door burst open and the universally accepted sound of John Q. Law chambering a shell into a shotgun rang out so loud Duke Ellington must have shit his pants. I may have been a sheet or two to the wind but there was no mistaking that voice shouting out, "Everybody show us your hands!"

I dove from my seat, taking along Nadine who was right behind me as did Doc Beaufort and Milly. We huddled beneath the card table as Grinder found his way to the floor. Thinking back, Grinder probably would have been on the floor anyway. But when gunshots began rat tat tatting, I knew one of Capone's henchman had the old Tommy gun do the talking as big Al slipped away. The scientists and business folk scurried about as the man with the shotgun shouted again: "Where are those vermin?...Beaufort you son of a bitch show yourself!

Beaufort climbed up from the ground and looked across the table seconds later my eyes were level with the felt and the glasses with the swizzle sticks. I watched as Beaufort grabbed his bejeweled swizzler, the stone glistened in the swinging overhead light. Al Capone must have taken mine and the man with the shotgun fired, missing Capone but not before the swizzle stick he must have swiped from my glass left his hands as he ran for the back door. The Sheriff grabbed it. I stared at Royal Wilkens dice cube teeth smile as he marvelled at what he'd come for.

Beaufort stood up and held out his swizzle stick and like that the atmosphere in the room began to change. The cops with Wilkens looked around, their guns readied but not really aimed at anything. Something had changed and the world seemed to have undergone some shift. The floor rumbled as if an earthquake was about to swallow us all and the lights began to flicker. A collective sigh from the partyers heaved so heavily the malevolent stench nearly killed us all. But that was nothing compared to the hiss and crackle of all things electrical and what began as a slight hiss escalated to a razzling burst of jolts of electricity which shot across the room sporardically zapping one person or another. Not a flapper, or gangster, or a scientist, or millionaire, it just buzzed, cackled, catapulted about the ballroom finally vectoring in on the swizzle sticks where a continuous duel between two lightning like bolts seemed to do battle. By now the static electricity became active and everyone in the room's hair stood on end. Al Einstein didn't look any different, but all the hair doo's of all the flappers went berserk. Buttons flew off shirts and clothing, zippers were strewn about in some cyclone of electricity that seemed more frantic than a battlefield whose combatants were made of pure energy itself. Beaufort's body had an aura of sorts as if it was an electrically charged planet. As did that of Royal Wilkens the Sheriff, the funky T.B.I. crook who wanted no more than to serve his own needs was fighting Beaufort over something I didn't understand, but felt every cell in my body may regret. The sounds in the room escalated from the electrical hum to a crescendo of high pitched, deafening frequencies that were as maddening as the Siren's Odysseus must have heard when he passed through the straits on his odyssey. But this wasn't Homer's tale and the man behind the bar knew it. I stood up and saw him standing on the bar, a huge pail in his hands, he looked at me and then at the dueling maniacs exchanging lightning bolts. The man whom The Proprietor called Negro Jim took that bucket and in one continuous motion hurled it's contents at the combatants. At that moment the world exploded into a billion blinding lights that may have been cosmic snowflakes, fireworks from Hades or some form of matter. After a second or so of molten white light rain, this lava of life or death, all things came to an end. And that was the last thing I remembered of 1928.

TO THE FUTURE

2070

I awoke with an unbelievable headache unaware of where I was or how I had gotten there. I did not know if I had been dreaming or just wished that I were. Slowly my senses returned and I could feel that my fingers and toes wiggled and even though I was afraid to open my eyes, I did. Things were blurry but I did hear a voice.

I opened my eyes and the outlines of reality seemed to fill in with the familiar figures and faces.

I was in a white room which was oddly familiar my memory must have been playing tricks on me, or I couldn't align my senses for one reason or another. Time travel. Make a note, not for sissies. Not for slobs either with the white everything everywhere I felt like I was floating. Maybe even barfing. I have to admit that I did feel queasy.

Doc Beaufort was grinning in that Cheshire Cat manner reserved for Sufi Masters, magician's, after a great performance, or a Maestro, who'd just conducted a fine orchestra.

"Welcome to the future, CP. Now your in my time." Beaufort tucked a little device into some pocket and raised his outstretched palms. "I don't think we'll have a lot of time right now to chat. Milly and I will be leaving you soon."

"Where's Nadine and Grinder?"

"They'll be along soon. Not to worry, just listen." Doc Beaufort said.

"What about the Sheriff? Won't he try and kill me again?"

"Now now, CP, old Sheriff Wilkens will be around soon enough. What do you think, Milly?"

"Beauf, I've got to agree. It may take a spell though, but he will, I assure you CP, be around." Her tone was ominous.

"What happened at the card game?" I asked.

"Someone won." Beaufort said. "But all went as it was intended. Jim did what he had to do. And that was all that could be done. Because if it didn't we wouldn't be having this little talk."

"But the swizzle sticks?" I said.

"Well they've landed exactly where they were intended to be. In the hands of Edison and later Henry Ford, Harvey Firestone, and Nikola Tesla. They did figure out a way to use it and that my good man is how the future was financed. That check engine light thing that goes off in automobiles since the 1980s? Everytime that luminous little thing goes off some imbecile goes to a mechanic who pays a fee of sorts, a tax if you will, to <u>The Organization</u>."

"Are you saying that nothing has changed? That the duel at Cap's place was just a meeting?"

"No. Not at all," Beaufort said. "The future was changed before that. Or maybe I should say, after that."

"What are you saying Doc?" I asked.

"I didn't want to tell you this, but that little incident where the deputy inspected your shoes set off a chain of events. That resulted in changes in the way foot gear was designed and how foot problems were treated. But as much as things may have changed some things have remained the same and there is still something you need to do." Beaufort said.

"Do what?" I said. "When can I see Nadine and Grinder?"

"When you awake," Doc Beaufort said. He had a small object in his hand.

"Why are just you and Milly here? Something did happen and you aren't telling me Doc. I need to know!"

"I like to call it a rapid transport and time shuf..." Doc Beaufort said, nodding his head. "Yep, an RT and a TS. Don't get to do that very often, but it sure feels good. What you say there Milly?"

"I like it fine, Beauf. I like it just fine I do." Milly had her arm draped over Doc Beaufort's shoulders and smiled in that knowing way that co-pilot's do at the pilot after they've accomplished some great feat. Or maybe a happily married couple does at any given time for any silly old reason or no reason at all.

I'd say that things were beginning to make sense, but that would be a lie. I wasn't sure just what had happened but based upon what already did occur nothing would surprise me. At least not then.

Suddenly there was a knock on the door. But there wasn't any door at all and Grinder stumbled in followed by Nadine, who must have given him a shove.

"Hello, CP," she said. "Welcome to 2070."

"Hi, Nadine."

"Did Doc Beaufort or Milly tell you that we're under house arrest?" she said.

HOUSE ARREST

So here we were, prisoners of sorts in a future that may or may not have been our future. What had happened,? What had become of the world as I thought I'd known it? My ordinary life became superfluous. My warranty had long since expired and the time I was in did not belong to me at all bothered me. How did I die, or did I die? What exactly happened at that crazy card game in 1928?

Did I disappear, evaporate or just go off the radar as some missing person? If I did, would there be other missing persons who'd fallen into the vortex of time, slipped perhaps accidentally into some iteration of a cornfield somewhere else, some time else? Would I meet Natalee Holloway? A Roman Centurion? A cave dweller? So many questions, yet oddly those questions didn't seem as pressing as to what had happened to the earth. Was there still an America? A political system? Had there been a grand war that decimated society? Did the terrorists take over? How many advances had taken place? It was as if I were a child on Christmas morning and each moment another gift to open, a glimpse into what had become either by some twist of fate, or grand design my place in time.

"They got any booze here?" Grinder was patting himself down. "I need a drink."

"Well, well, well, I don't know if I can rightly answer some of your questions due to the fact that the knowledge you glean may very well change what you discover."

"What's that supposed to mean?" I said.

"What Doc Beaufort is saying is that you can't stay here. The future isn't for anyone to know." Milly said.

We were in our cell, the white room. A white, white, white, room with white curtains, and white sofas. And no matter what it was, we were prisoners. Everything in the room was made of a material that was...wait! Holy crap we were in Beaufort's nineteen fifty eight office only everything was white.

"I'm truly sorry, boys, but you're going to have to remain in this room for a spell. I have to get to the T.B.I. and make my report. If it's still there and if the same folks are still running it. Who knows what those collsarn orthotics and running shoes had done? It's imperative I get in to see the nanotechnicians and have a few adjustments made."

"What about the Sheriff?" I asked.

"The Sheriff is not permitted to return to this time until his tour of the past has expired. For now he's going to be conducting his search throughout human history."

"That's a bit long, isn't it?"

"Well, well, well, those tracking devices you have installed in your bodies will shortly be scrambled to the extent that Sheriff Wilkens will be chasing a White Rabbit. He'll be heading toward the French Revolution for a spell, a few hours in Nazi occupied Czechoslovakia, and maybe a swing though Hurricane Andrew. That should keep him busy until your nanotrackers are tuned and you pass through the old nanotechtonic rejuvenators a few times. Yep, you two will be good for years and the Sheriff, hehehe, he's going to be sent on a wild duck chase."

"Goose chase," I said. "You mean goose chase."

"No son, I mean duck. He's going to be doing a lot of ducking where he's going."

"How long will that keep him off our asses?"

"Until he figures out what's happened and corrects it. Sort of like the Check Engine Light on an automobile. Hehehehe, he'll know something's awry but it'll take a spell till he figures out what it is."

"Really?" I said. "That's pretty cool."

"We call it a time shuffle. Not quite the ethical thing to do but, for Wilkens..." Beaufort shrugged. "What can I say? I believe that scoundrel's earned a little trouble of his own."

"What about you and Milly?"

"What about us? We'll go back to 1958 and pick up where we left off. Unless of course something goes awry."

"Will I see you guys again?"

"Well, well, well, we never know what the future will bring even if its in the past," he said.

"No matter what," Nadine said, "don't try to leave this room."

"No." Beaufort agreed. "Don't try to escape. What will be is meant to be."

Nadine spoke up: "Listen, CP, I have to go with Beaufort and Milly back to 1958 to pass through the rejuvinator in THAT TIME so I can join you in THIS time. Don't worry, I'll be back.

"Wait a second," I said. "Why can't we go with you?"

"It doesn't work that way, son." Beaufort said.

"Hey," I said, "I'm not your son..." but before I could finish the sentence I heard a soft pop.

And with that, Nadine, Beaufort and Milly vanished as if they were never there.

I often wondered what the future would hold. Would there be resolution of grand geopolitical issues? Peace in the Middle East? A robust economy? Had human beings evolved to a point where they could communicate with each other without hostility? Had there been a nuclear war, or worse? Doc Beaufort said something to that effect but was vague as to who won or lost and what were the cell phone wars he'd alluded to? What were the politics of this time? Who was in charge, if anyone at all? Were humans in two thousand seventy part man part machine? What and who was the T.B.I.? Who or what enforced the laws if there were any at all?

And health and sickness? Doctors and hospitals? I did glean from my conversations with Doc Beaufort back in nineteen fifty eight and again in nineteen seventy eight that human beings had figured out a way to cure most disease and live extraordinarily long lives. But did aliens visit the planet? Was there still racism, bigotry, and all the things I'd been aware of back in my times? How much money accumulated in the account I set up after winning the `78 Kentucky Derby? And investing in the mutual fund? Had to be a tidy sum. But would it still be there? How would I find out? Damn, there was so much I wanted to know about life in 2070. But here we were stuck in that white room waiting.

There was a barely audible tap at the non door. We were surprised and looked away from our activities, fortunately guys like Grinder and I knew how to piss away time. We were actually quite good at it. Killing time, that is. Then again with time travel and all it might be some sort of crime to be abusive of time itself. But the fact that someone came by made me start to think some answers were forthcoming. I don't recall precisely how many games of rock, paper, scissors, Grinder and I played but my hands were sore from getting slapped and slapping. By about the four thousandth paper wraps around rock and slap from Grinder to my knuckles.

Someone poked their head in the door. It was a pasty skinned blond haired woman in a white body suit. She said: "Hello, gentlemen, my name is Lucerva and I have been sent here to satisfy your needs." Her accent was almost non existent, but if I was asked to describe it, I'd have to say it was a cross between the please fasten your seat belt voice of a nineteen ninety nine Volvo, or a right passenger door is open voice of a 2008 Jaguar. Tough to tell. Maybe she was an android. I forgot that Grinder could read thoughts and he had a shit eating smirk on his face.

"Maybe she's a sperminator."

"Shut the fuck up, Grinder," I said and then looked over at the woman.

"Yo," Grinder said, grabbing his crotch.

The woman was attractive in that mannequin sort of way, cold yet pleasant and she did have a degree of sensibility that confirmed my notions that certain forms of of idiocy defy the passage of time.

"Pardon me?" She beamed at Grinder, who shrugged his shoulders and bowed his head like a teenager caught smoking in the boys room with his pants down.

Lucerva turned to face me and shot a quick shake of her head as if she was at the edge of saying shut the hell up you moron to Grinder but was sent here to accommodate us, just doing her job.

Looking back I do not recall precisely how or why we, Grinder and I, were foolish enough to have not taken heed to Doc Beaufort's instructions to remain in the white room. But the thrill, the utter excitement that enveloped every ingram of my being became manifest as we emerged from whatever receptacle we were in, to a world so foreign to us that it may have been as if we were on another planet entirely. There were portions of the white room covered with curtains, which Grinder shuffled about until he discovered that there were no windows at all, rather soft spots, actually mushy spots in the wall where windows should have been. He gingerly placed a finger, then a hand into the gelatinous mass, pulled it out to discover no harm or residue, he finally shoved his face into the rubbery, almost Jello-like portal. I watched him lean there, his head immersed in the wall up to his shoulders. I must say that Grinder looked like some pervert peeping through a fence as Becky Thatcher undressed behind her window.

And just like that he yanked his head out of the unwindow and whipped his head around. The portal shut with a hushed snap that sounded like a farting cat, and made the wall appear as if it were just like an ordinary wall. Grinder had a smile on his face like he'd just swallowed a canary.

"Mother fucker!" he said. "You got to see this. It's the fucking future, man. I've seen the fucking future and it's now." He had his hand out, motioning me to come over to the wall and peek through. "I'm crawlin' out there, it's friggin' un-mother-fucking-believable, man."

I hung back, held my palms up to Grinder and if I recall precisely even took a step back. I was afraid. I was afraid that seeing the future might change the past. After all we had no business knowing what the future had become and knowing it, might change what we'd become. I looked at Grinder and was about to tell him this when he shot back in a flurry of words and thoughts: "There's nothing that is, that already was. The fact we're here is a fluke so you ain't got nothin' to lose by seein' what's happening now. Shit, we don't know if it's even possible for us to go back to when, right?"

After a few beats, I had to agree. What the fuck?

We were standing outside of an oblong shaped structure that could have been a building of sorts, a freight container, or a space ship. I'd never seen the likes of anything similar to it before. Not in any movie, or TV show, or picture, depicting any future I could ever imagine. I placed my palm against it, cool to the touch, and ran my hand across the surface, finding the mushy entry-exit non-gunk portal, door or whatever it was called and looked over at Grinder who was maybe a foot away from me. Behind him was a terrain unlike anything imaginable even by minds who'd made up the coolest of cool time travel stories. The sky was a crisp cornflower blue and was more clear than a sky could be. In fact its color was hypnotizing in its clarity and the fact is what really hit me like a kick to the head, there were two half moons, maybe yay by yay apart. Don't ask me how far a yay is because there was no way to determine physical principles, weights, and measures, or any kind I could know of in a world where there was no gravity. No gravity whatsoever in a way that I'd come to know gravity. It was as if some power or force kept our feet off the ground. This was a technology of sorts, designed I figured to protect the earth, maybe from time travelers like us or just as a matter of course for this place in time. I did not know at the moment, nor did I care. As to who or what ever was in charge puzzled me, and I was curious as to why and how someone or something had figured out a way to do this, to control gravity. Neal Grinder, as he stood before me was about a foot above the ground and could walk a few feet right or left on the atmosphere, the air, the whatever the fuck it was without touching the ground. It was as if he was suspended by some invisible path that seemed more to protect the ground more than it did his feet. And the ground was perfect. The lawn looked like the putting green of some divine golf course and looking up and beyond Grinder was a grand fairway stretching out forever like an Infinity pool. In the distance there was a bit of farm land and then a skyline of sorts, a cluster of outrageous structures. Buildings of sorts that reminded me of an M.C. Escher drawing that Salvador Dali toyed around with. Precise, surreal architecture meant that humanity in one form or another survived and thrived. I wanted to know more. I recalled Beaufort speaking about some wars and developments in medicine and science. And I felt a desire to forge on a need like none I'd known before to find out the forbidden knowledge. Yes, I was like a kid with a gift-wrapped package and I'd just yanked off the ribbon.

Grinder smiled at me. Maybe it was the atmosphere that made him jubilant, almost buzzed, but I felt it too. "Hey, what the hell?" And we walked a foot or so above the beautiful lawn toward the present which was in every sense of our world, the future. Shit, it was confusing getting my tenses straight.

So here we are.

"Let's check it out," I said to Grinder. "What are they gonna do to us?"

"If these guys is so friggin' smart you think they got some kinda torture or punishment. Shit, man. These gotta be some civilized motherfuckers. Let's go check it out. I bet the bars here are un-fucking believable." I shrugged, grinned and said, "What the hell?

OFF TO SEE THE WIZARD

"What are you doing?" A woman's voice. It wasn't spoken aloud, but it could have been. It was a telepathic message which was different from those telepathies and mind reading abilities that'd been bestowed upon us by Doc Beaufort. I'd like to say all those years ago, but it wasn't, at least to me an all those years thing. It, time that is, was contorted, twisted, bent, curved, and disallowed, for any explanation I could make sense of. But telepathy. Maybe I didn't really consider delving into any description of it on account of all the other madness that happened. So here goes...

HOW MIND READING AND MENTAL TELEPATHY CAN BE A PAIN IN THE ASS...

You'd think that if you could read minds it'd be pretty cool, right? Totally wrong. It's like you can hear with your mind's ears every freaking thought within some ill defined proximity you're in. And if you happen to be in a crowd? Fuggedaboutit. I haven't been to an insane asylum, but I did see a movie a few years ago that depicted someone in a madhouse hearing the hollers and screams of all the loonies. I guess there was a manual of sorts, or a course that was given when this technology or stage in the evolutionary process became manifest in a society in the future. But I wasn't there yet. When it began, it was thrust upon me, and I savored reading Nadine's thoughts, maybe that way of communicating with her sparked the romance and all that ensued between us. But this isn't some lecherous litany and you pervs reading this, chill out. Women have a whole different way of thinking than men. That's the first thing I learned. Men, who've just acquired the skill, like Grinder and I, usually think a shitload of things that are in the old X-rated zone as well as a few, at least in my case, mindful meanderings. Grinder? Shit, he's really a twisted son of a bitch. But that's a different story. As you catch on to the whole mind reading thing it becomes apparent that you can not read, pick up, or interpret, every thought someone has. Future people imbued with this ability have a way of editing and censoring what they think and projecting only those thoughts they want to have read. So nix any notion you're going to win a poker game in the future or get a read on someone you've just met. Nope. Don't work that way. If I want to project a thought, I have to hold it in my conscious mind in that, as if I'm about to say it aloud, mode. That is how you do it. And as to the cacophony of all the maddening voices and terrors and wildly screeching thoughts people think, you pick up pretty quickly on how you can simply tune them out. Yeah, it takes a little practice, but you DO find a balance and every prefrontal cortical impulse doesn't turn into a tri fi front row seat at a bad concert. Now the really cool thing about it is the level of intimacy you can have with someone. I mean Nadine and I sort of knew each others thoughts in a way I'd never known. Was it a novelty? Hell yes!

Would I really want to have been able to read the minds of most of the people I'd known throughout my life. No. People, and I can best reflect on the folks I've met since having this ability, like Chalk and Tamina and Grinder and the store clerk in nineteen seventy eight...they're in some ways disturbing. Do you really want to know when someone is saying to themselves: "I wonder if it's all right to fart now? Will it smell?" You catch my drift?

That reminded me that it'd been a while since my last meal. Even longer since my last drink.

BACK TO LUCERVA'S MIND TOSS AND ESCORT

Lucerva had come upon us like she'd been transported by some starship beaming device.

Grinder nudged me. "She's got a nice bod in that white Spandex get up. Huh?"

"Shut the fuck up," I said. The white body suit wasn't that simple of an outfit, it was an elaborate form fitting diving suit sort of thing that had a network of embedded computer chip looking patterns all over it and looked like Rand McNally'd gone blotto with a box of computer guts putting together a three D getup.

Now what struck me most, wasn't just being in an uncertain future, but the fact that we should not have been here at all was maddening. Yet here we were, and whatever or wherever it was, we had to follow some rules. We had strict instructions to remain in the White Room.

"Yes, you did," Lucerva projected. "But since you've managed to get out. I have to make sure that you don't contaminate our world." She looked down at the anti-grav strut about devices Grinder and I stood elevated above the earth on. "You cannot leave a footprint here. It will change an already disrupted space-time continuum."

"What the fuck's this broad talkin' about, CP?"

"I don't know." I said.

"Look at the earth beneath us. It is untouched by our body mass. The area we are approaching is most delicate."

"Lady, you're pretty delicate," Grinder said.

Ignoring him, she continued. "If you notice that we are above a field of corn is because the stalks of corn not only are a precious resource but serve as the ideal resonance reflectors to relocate and transfer our people throughout time."

I didn't say anything-just took it all in.

We seemed to be scootering over the earth faster and faster finally reaching the outskirts of the city of tomorrow which was today. Lucerva surged ahead of us, pivoted, turned to face Grinder and I and held up a hand in the universal halt gesture.

"This is Enopolis. There are rules here. Different rules apply to different people from different times. One rule that you must abide by is that you cannot hold a thought in your head longer than the most brief of moments that pertains to your past or you will feel a jolt."

"What the fuck's she talkin' about?" Grinder asked.

At the very moment the words were thought, spoken, or expressed, either in his head or uttered verbally a jolt of some motherfucking thing kicked in and sent Grinder into a soundless scream as he clutched his head with his palms pressed against his ears.

"The populated portions of our world are surrounded by impulse and thought deflectors which respond to any hostile, biophysiologic, neural, impulses remotely resembling something that would be the fight or flight mechanism."

"So if you get pissed off you get brain smacked by some computer program?" I said, trying to remain calm. I didn't want to get brain smacked. I looked at Grinder who had a look on his face like a dog that shit the rug and his master smacked his snout.

"Yes." Lucerva said. "After a span of time you learn..."

"Define a span of time," I said.

"Yeah," Grinder said. "Tell us what or how time is measured? I ain't no Pavlovian pigeon" He said it indignantly and I wondered if he'd get zapped again.

I didn't have a clue as to how they told time in a place where people could travel about in leaps and bounds through years and decades so easily.

"Tell us, please." I said calmly. "How do you measure time these days."

"In bursts," she said holding out what may have been wristwatches but they weren't. "Place them on your wrists and look at them. One burst is the period it takes to go from one experience to another. Time as you've known it is not measured as it was from where you came from. It is measured in experiences tied in to your metabolism, thought processes, and by the implanted nucleotide its respective protein markers and reflected by your impulse meter." She held hers up.

"Shit, I gotta think nice thoughts and some computer is reading my mind directing me in one fercockta way or another. Is this how shit works in these parts, we're fucking slaves to those bullshit nanotechtonic whatever the fuck reboobinators Beaufort put in us, huh?"

"Grinder, cool it. You wanna get another zap?"

But I was too late. The words did not form quick enough.

Again Grinder had another jolt and clutched his head.

"He's catching on," she said. "Frankly I did not think that your friend was that quick on the pick up."

Looking back, actually it would have been looking forward I would have cracked wise and said she was a smug bitch. But at that point I knew better and just shut my thoughts and my mouth the hell up.

"Yes, this is how things work in these parts. And yes, you should keep your thoughts and words to yourself. I am a smug bitch. Try not to forget that."

So we continued to hover toward the thick of things. Here we were in the future. I was wondering just as Grinder was, where a watering hole was and maybe find an ATM machine, or whatever permutation of those were in twenty seventy. Eh. I'd best keep my thoughts to myself until something turns up. That's about when it occurred to me that us breaking out of the white room and the gal, Lucerva, showing up to guide us was a set up. A flat out set up as if we'd been expected to behave as we did. But I didn't dare think it. Nope. No brainsmacking for me.

IN THE CITY

The humans were going about their business to'ing and fro'ing as if some grand orchestra played an elaborate symphony as their background music. There were cars but they were flying cars and other people on the streets that were not streets at all rather pathways of sorts that no one seemed to walk on, rather above. And shops. Yes, there are shops in the future. My tense becomes addled because I was there then, which was a now and I may be there later.

Lucerva ushered us the way an escort might, but didn't use a hand at all. Rather she used her mind to grab our intellectual elbows and herd us into the lobby of a building. The structure could have been anything from a bank, or post office, to haberdashery, on account every building looked the same. Frank Lloyd Wright would've keeled over on the street, but; in 2070 you weren't allowed to even touch the streets. So far the future really sucked the way it is, was, or will be-I don't, didn't or won't know until it gets there. But at that moment when Lucerva had us in this building we saw a riveting, wavy piece of signage appear as if she'd just thought it up revealing the names of people occupying this place. Lucerva looked at it, then over at Grinder. I looked at the directory Grinder was staring at her ass.

"Stop staring at my ass," she said.

At that Grinder got another brainsmack.

"If you continue to behave or think in the manner which you do, the impulse detectors will disable some of your most favorable bodily functions."

"What's he gonna shit the floor?" I said. At that it was as if a jolt of lightning struck the ground right next to me and every fucking cell in my body squirted out enough epinephrine to power a pro ball team toward a field goal. My head felt like an explosion went off and the shards of bright lights in my head stuck to the roof of my skull just long enough to be reminded NOT to think one thought or another. Shit, this is the future? This fucking mind control crap sucked big fucking time-damn, dare I think that thought? I did but nothing happened. I guess nothing happened on account that I didn't think it too hard and maybe the fact that some thoughts were still fermented in all the years of boozing and guzzling Sterno. Well maybe that was a good thing I thought softly and looked over at the woman in white. Fucking pasty skin blond bitch. No, I was beginning to not like this broad very much. I was just wondering when the next brain smack would arrive.

"Pay attention," she said. Reading, no doubt my thoughts.

"We are going to visit someone."

"Who?" I asked.

She nodded at the shimmering directory. There were the names of a whole bunch of entities, most of them lawyers but there were a few individuals with titles and degrees after their names I could only pretend to imagine what they meant. And just like that, the sign disappeared and Lucerva pivoted to face us.

"I know you know where your taking us. Why the big show as if you've never been here?" I said.

"I have not been to the city for a long time. This sort of anomaly is unusual." She looked us over. "Stragglers of sorts from the past usually don't end up with an awareness of where they are."

"Lady, I don't know where the hell I am." Grinder said.

"Precisely. That's why I am taking you to see a familiar."

"A familiar?" I said and shrugged my shoulders.

"Yes, someone you may have known in your time as someone from this time who moved back to a place in time where they had probably vacationed at one time and decided to move there."

"Time travel vacations." I milled this notion over in my mind.

"It's very common and popular. Has been for a decade. Many who can afford to relocate do so. I think you will recognize the fellow we'll be visiting."

OFFICE VISIT

So there I stood face to face with Tommy Brassiter who had not aged a day since I'd last seen him in 2012, I understood the meaning of relocation. He still wore a leather jacket and an Elvis Presley hair doo but he wasn't any one I'd know as an osteopath or who he'd been before that. When Grinder and I had seen him last, at his office on our way to Hoogerstown he was a blustery bandit pushing pills and and scamming insurance companies faster than you can travel through time in a cornfield. Grinder stood like a statue, not a thought in his usually rambling skull. Lucerva had her hands behind her back like a sentinel as we stood in the very plain, very no nonsense suite in a very tall structure in the year 2070.

"Hey guys," Tommy said. "Glad to see you made it."

"Made it? We're you expecting us?" I said.

"I certainly could not have let you and Grinder make it over to the, uh..nursing home could I?"

"What the fuck are you talkin' about Tommy? We thought you were cool, we had some laughs you gave us some Vicodin, we had drinks?" Grinder said.

"Guys," Tommy walked around his floating desk and motioned for us to relax. "Those were not Vicodin."

"I knew they were beat." Grinder said. "What the fuck did you give us?"

"I had to prep your bodies for the …"

"For the what Tommy? What the fuck's going on here?" I said.

"Calm down CP," Lucerva said in that cool check engine light tone. That foreboding utterance did not calm me. No not at all. I was expecting a brain smack, but it didn't come.

"Listen, things are not what you think." Tommy said.

"And what do I think, huh, Tommy? Because if you had one idea of what I was thinking your sorry ass would be running down the fucking hallway and shit and piss would be running down your leg. Asshole."

"It sure is nice that you good old boys found your way over," someone said from a huge chair in one of the room's furthest corners. I knew that voice. I couldn't see him, but he was sitting in the chair facing the wall. The voice struck me the way a shot of over proof rum does when it hits your stomach. The tone of the speaker was in that easy pitch and cadence used by commercial pilots to tell us how safe we'd be upon arriving at our destination. Telling us, to put our trays up, and move our seats to an upright position. It had that sound of authority reserved for law enforcement or some cool calm adversary who knew they'd won the match before it was over. I didn't have to put two and two together to know who said: "the room's sealed from the impulse detectors." Royal Wilkens said. "There's not going to be much mind reading in here. And now I've got you just where you belong." He turned to face us and the gun in his hand was the same weapon he had in 1978. It was cocked and I knew that he had every intention to kill us dead on the spot.

"I am going to finish you boys off," Wilkens continued. "Just as I am going to eliminate Doc Beaufort, Milly and Nadine. They moved into my territory in 1958. That was OK, but then you and your buddy showed up. They, Beaufort, Milly, and Nadine, coddled you. They told you about the future, and implanted you with the mymine nucleotide and nanotechtonic rejuvenators. You and Grinder changed the future. In 1978 you did it again with Chalk. Who do you think owns this building? That's right, Chalk does. And Duss, the chiropodist? Too many changes along the way."

"You're deck was shuffled by Beaufort, you were supposed to be scrapping about through time and history..." I said.

"Please. It only took a few minutes to disengage that nano shuffle. The Organization has way too much invested in me to let something as petty as a time shuffle last very long."

"What about the T.B.I.?" I said.

Wilkens smiled revealing those dice cube teeth and said: "There is no T.B.I.; you changed all that in 1978. You invested in a mutual fund which should have failed. It didn't, and the funds went to you, and other investors who backed another candidate. Your lousy investment grew making too many too rich, and a lot money was poured into opponents of our cause. That superseded a presidential election, and the wrong guy got into office. You're very existence has been a bane on my life. And now, it's time for all of you to die."

"Wait a second. What about Doc Beaufort, Milly and Nadine. Where are they?"

"They're perfectly safe for now they're in the year 1958. They have to be killed in 1958 before you ever had a chance to meet them. They're being held in a ready room to be transported as soon as you've been vanquished, CP."

"Sorry, old sport," Tommy said. "You've upset the scheme of things. That nursing home wasn't a nursing home at all. It was a laboratory that was set up by The Organization and Wilkens job is, was, and will always be, to keep the likes of guys like you and Grinder away."

"What's this guy's like you shit?" Grinder said.

Tommy waved a dismissive hand and continued.

"And you, you bums were going to stumble upon it. I couldn't let that happen."

"Are you sayin' we was set up?" Grinder said.

"No, you were never set up for anything. You just were at the wrong place at the wrong time," Lucerva said.

Tommy Brassiter interrupted: "Listen, CP, I went back years ago. I was set. Set for life and then some. Then you guys stumbled in, shit, you were supposed to have died in that accident."

"So you knew this all along?"

"Actually it was <u>The</u> <u>Organization</u>," Tommy said.

"Enough of the fucking <u>Organization</u>. The Organi-fucking-zation is shit. It's just assholes like you, Tommy, like Wilkens and other dickbrains who get whatever the fuck they want and become its slaves and you Tommy, you're just another fucking slave you sonofabitch." I was pissed off. Really fucking fuming to the point where I didn't care much for predetermination or destiny and my own fate was in MY fucking hands.

My blood was boiling and my chest felt like a race horse had gone mad, its hooves kicking against its stall-my chest. My throat was as dry as my ex-wife's crotch. I stared at Wilkens with pupils dilated, fixed and aflame with hatred. I wanted to throttle the son of a bitch, ordinarily some impulse control mechanism would kick in, but it didn't. My lizard brain took over and my hypothalmus went into overdrive sending signals to my adrenals and the adrenaline flowed like an angry volcano. Even though he had a gun, that part of my mind to see it for what it was, shut down. I don't know why, but the world switched into slow motion and I could see myself in my mind's eye dive toward Grinder just as Sheriff Wilkens discharged his firearm. Tommy and Lucerva were behind the now standing Wilkens and he was taking aim again, this time the gun was pointed right at Grinder's forehead whose mind was void of thought, like the proverbial deer in the headlights. He stood there ready to be slaughtered. I grabbed something, to this day I don't know why, but I knew at the time it had some heft, and hurled it toward Wilkens. It must have struck him in a vulnerable spot because he took a step back and grabbed his face. At that moment I was on him, I wrapped my right arm around his waist and squeezed tightly, forcing him against the wall, the gun fired again skyward. "Grinder," I yelled out. "Grab the gun!"

I wrestled Wilkens down and had him on his back. He was unusually light for a man his size but that didn't matter-I didn't know what to do other than pick up what I'd thrown at him. I was going to smash his face but thought I'd better look at it. Wilkens was too stunned at what had just happened so were Lucerva and Tommy B. By then Grinder had the gun in his shaky hands and held it out toward the Sheriff.

I stared at my trusty Sterno bottle and knew just what had to be done. I used my teeth to pull off the cap and thrust the bottle's neck into Wilken's mouth. He tried not to open wide, but I kneed him in the nuts. He yelped, I poured. I knew damn well what I was doing. The additional cyclic nucleotide, mymine, would be deactivated with a rapid change in the body's pH and this might be some serious shit for Wilkens. Not more than a few seconds after the few drops dribbled down his throat, his eyes bulged out and he gasped. I stood up, holding the Sterno at my side. I watched Wilkens. I thought he'd aged faster than the guy at the end of that Indiana Jones movie.

Within a half-minute he'd be nothing other than a pile of ashes. That wasn't the case.

"His mymine is destroyed." Lucerva said. "Now he's just out cold. He won't be making any time trips for a while."

"Now you've done it, CP." Brassiter said. "Give me the gun Grinder. You fucked up history."

"I don't think so Tommy. I think we fucked up YOUR fucking history!" Grinder pointed the weapon at Tommy and then at Lucerva. "Now who's your daddy bitches? Huh? How you like me now?" Grinder was smiling.

"He's right, bee yatches," I said. "And now you're going to take us to Nadine, Beaufort, and Milly."

"Oh yeah," Tommy said. "Or what?"

Grinder fired the weapon. A bullet whizzed over Tommy B's right shoulder. "Then we end you, asshole."

"You know, Tommy, I always thought you were an asshole. Now I know it. You and blondie here can knock yourselves out contemplating the fact that today may very well have been your day to die."

We herded them toward the door.

"I really hope you give me a reason to shoot you," Grinder said.

"Why's that, Neal? I always liked you." Tommy Brassiter said softly.

"Well I never liked osteopaths, and you and that smarmy tone. I might just decide to leave you crippled just for the fuck of it."

"Why would you do that?" Lucerva said.

"Because, sweetheart, that's the way we do it where I come from," Grinder snarled.

She started to say something, I could sense the thought impulse form in her mind but she held it back. "All right. We'll take you to them."

"You're lives depend on it." I added, using my most menacing voice, despite the fact I was scared shitless.

We were in the hover car, which was also impulse detector proofed and rode in silence as the cornfield beneath us, and the cityscape behind us was in the distance. Tommy was driving and Lucerva sat in the passenger seat, both of them unsure as to what would become of them. The structure we'd escaped from was standing there where we'd left it.

"Where the fuck else would it be," Grinder said, breaking the silence.

At that, Tommy jerked the controls and we came crashing down. Everything faded to black and the last thing I recalled was the world rushing by in a flurry and then, nothing. Not one thing at all.

THE PRESENT IS NOW

I awoke today, a bit earlier than usual. There were no sounds on the bridge. Maybe it was Sunday or there was some roadwork somewhere along the artery into and out of Big Town. Maybe. But the air, the air was brisk, fresh and crisp. I smelled coffee, not stale beer, urine and dried vomit. The world, my world was much different from what I'd recalled on any other morning. My dreams though, they were more vivid, their colors didn't dissipate as I began to move about and like ordinary mornings, my dreams lingered even as I made my way to the convenience store, addling down the concrete embankment I could see Nell, the mini-skirted hooker. I could just make out her features in the pewter predawn light.

There was something about her that was different. In fact there was something different about the whole neighborhood. The convenience store was gone. There was a park of sorts and a fountain in its center. There were elegant copper benches which looked like they belonged in an English garden along with the hedgerows and ornate street lamps. As the sun climbed higher I could see through the orange and amber light the outline of a Disneyworld like monorail where there once stood a rail yard that'd gone into disarray. The shops, what had once been an array of boarded up graffitti filled wrecks were high end stores. I stared at the Tiffany's, the Cartier, and Burberry's shops flanked by Chanel, a Gallery, which upon closer inspection had an exhibit of Kandinsky, Rothko and Pollack-must've been over eight million in artwork in one store alone. What the fuck? Where was I?

Nell must have seen the look of puzzlement on my face because she walked over to me and said: "Hey CP, are you all right?" No more street accent. She wasn't dressed as what I'd thought was a hooker. She had on an outfit that was right out of a fashion magazine. "You need some coffee." She said and at that I caught a waft of freshly brewed coffee and the rich smells of fresh bread.

"Where am I?" I said looking over toward the scent's that tickled my nose.

"You be home," Nell said. "What you doin' with your P.J.s on?"

I looked at myself and then back at where my digs beneath the bridge was supposed to be. I was wearing silk pajamas and the initials C.P. were monogrammed on my upper right torso. Where the crevice between concrete had been was a walkway leading toward a sprawling estate. What happened to Big Town?

Nell must have read my thoughts because she stared at me and shook her head. "You had it torn down and rebuilt, redeveloped the neighborhood years ago. Are you sure you're all right? Let's get you some coffee." She pointed her chin toward what used to be the place the bums and winos huddled about. They were gone.

There was an elegant little coffee shop where living breathing human beings sat outside sipping coffee, smiling, reading, staring at iThis or iThats off tiny tablets, and maybe there was a newspaper or two but that was about it.

My reverie was interrupted by something that sounded like a high pitched electric motor. What the...?"

At that moment a golf cart's brakes squealed like a screaming ex-wife and came to a rumbling halt. I whipped my head around and felt a jolt. The man behind the wheel turned to adjust the bags and clubs that'd gotten tossed about. I couldn't make out who it was at first. He wore an old-fashioned golfer's cap and had on bright green plaid slacks and a yellow cardigan. When he turned to face me, I looked at him and smiled: "Grinder?"

"What the hell are you doing?" he said, dismounting the cart. "Nadine's waiting for you up at the house."

"You'd best be getting along." Nell said.

"Wait a fucking second. I'm dreaming. This can't be real." I don't know why, but I ran toward the coffee shop and grabbed a newspaper from one of the tables. I looked at the date. Two thousand thirty five. The headlines read that the trans African Highway had finally been completed joining Europe to Africa. I looked around and the people at the cafe were staring at me. Must have been my pajamas.

"C'mon, get in the cart." Grinder said.

We'd driven for a few minutes down a long path of sorts which led to a red brick road and he stopped, looked both ways and said: "This friggin' driveway. Damn bricks always clip the tires of my ride dammit." He'd jerked the cart back into drive and we forged on. I looked around as the driveway led to a compound of sorts, there was a greenhouse off to the left and a stable to the right and a large circular driveway with a bunch of exotic cars parked there in front of a house. It was more Architectural Digest meets some University from a movie or a Four Seasons Hotel than house at first glance, but as we approached it had an eerily familiar, almost welcoming sense to it. It, the house that is, was a sumptuous, estate well manicured landscaping, yet quirky in a way only my minds eye could see. It looked as if it were something I'd made up in that part of my mind as to what a cool house would or should look like. So there I was trying to calculate how much it must cost to maintain. The lawn, rows of hedges. the exotic plants and flowers.

"This is really something, Grinder. Whose place is this?" I said, staring at the sprawling Tudor style house. We stopped the golf cart for a moment so Grinder could light up a smoke. I stared at the house marveling at how the nineteenth century ivy casually wrapped about the entire home in an envelope of sorts suggesting to me that whoever lived there had taken comfort in it.

"Hey, we're here," Grinder said. We'd pulled up to the front entry and the twin oak doors were closed. Grinder honked the horn of the cart. I didn't recall golf carts having horns, but this one did. And it had the tune Macho Man by the Village People. "What an asshole," I thought to myself.

"What the hell are you doing, Grinder?" I said.

"What are you, in space? You're home, man." Grinder flipped his butt on to the driveway. "And don't give me any shit about tossing cigarette butts out."

"I'm …"

At that moment one of the doors opened. A beautiful woman stepped out.

It was Nadine. She put her hands on her hips, smiled and said: "where've you been? Come on in, you must've been sleep walking."

"I guess I was," I said, and walked over to Nadine, put my arms around her and kissed her as though it was the first time and the thousandth time. She kissed me back. I felt her body against mine and the warmth between us felt as if we'd shared more than just a hug, something powerful, like we'd been together for a long time. I don't know how long the embrace lasted. Hell, it could have gone on forever; but it was interrupted by Grinder.

"Hey Caddypod, this letter showed up. Special delivery about an hour ago. It's old, looks like something from the fifties or so." Grinder held up the envelope and shook it like a Polaroid, then held it out.

"I'm going to fix you some breakfast CP, then I'll meet you in the boudoir." She smiled, winked and I watched her backside as it disappeared into the home as she headed toward the kitchen.

I sat down on one of the cement steps and opened the letter.

"Hey what's it say CP?" Grinder lit another cigarette and had his hand out as if he needed to know something that he probably already knew.

I took out a handwritten document. It was Ivory bond paper with a watermark and the lettering was perfect. It looked like it was written with a fountain pen. This is what it said:

Dear Caddypod,

I hope this letter finds you well,

It's never good to live in the past too long. And the future, well, the future is whatever you want it to be.

Feel free to drop in anytime, in time,

Your friends,

Doc Beaufort and Milly

To be continued...